I Belong To God

Elder Coco,
Thanks for the support!
Great to meet you!

I BELONG TO GOD:
Staying On The Christian Path to Success

By
Minister Jared Sawyer Jr.

Copyright © 2013 by Jared Sawyer Jr.
All rights reserved. No part of this book may be reproduced, scanned, or distributed in any printed or electronic form without permission.
First Edition: September 2013
Printed in the United States of America

I would like to dedicate this book to my great-grandfather, Deacon Freeman Blount, and my great-grandmother, Mother Ann Blount.

Freeman Blount
"Knowing that from the Lord you will receive the inheritance as your reward. You are serving the Lord Christ."
Colossians 3:24

Ann Blount
"She opens her mouth with wisdom, and the teaching of kindness is on her tongue."
Proverbs 31:26

CONTENTS

Introduction

CHAPTER ONE
  The Simplicity and Power of Prayer

CHAPTER TWO
  I Don't Mind Waiting On The Lord

CHAPTER THREE
  Standing Out > Fitting In

CHAPTER FOUR
  When There's Nothing Left But God

CHAPTER FIVE
  Putting God First

CHAPTER SIX
  There Is A Destiny Behind Your Experiences

CHAPTER SEVEN
  Forgive and Don't Forget, But Learn

CHAPTER EIGHT
  He's Still God

CHAPTER NINE
  A Personal Relationship With Jesus Christ

CHAPTER TEN
  Let God Fight Your Battles

CHAPTER ELEVEN
      Faith In The Right Place – Opportunities Like Never Before

CHAPTER TWELVE
      Be Humble – Don't Forget Your Roots

CHAPTER THIRTEEN
      Praise Towards Progress

CHAPTER FOURTEEEN
      Favor, Grace, and Mercy

CHAPTER FIFTEEN
      You Can Make It

Introduction

There is absolutely no doubt that we are living in a unique day in time – one that cannot be completely explained in the most of words and statements. We are living in a world that has a consistently variable status. Not one problem is a majority; more are minorities, as they sometimes feel countless from time to time.

Every time we turn around, we hear about something that is of bad nature. Every time we turn around we hear about something that is displeasing in the eyes of God. Every time we turn around someone is sick in their body, there is some type of mass man or natural disaster, or the rate for something detrimental has increased higher than ever before.

Every time we turn on the news, read the newspaper, or visit a popular homepage on the internet, there is some drama, problem, disaster or circumstance that we read. It is totally unarguable that times have surely changed and the truth is that they are continuing to change; but, they are not changing for the better. They are, instead, changing for the worse, rapidly throughout its course.

Life has never been easy for any individual, but it is definitely harder now than it has ever been in the past before. Failures appear to prevail over victories. Difficulties appear to prevail over eases. Enemies appear to prevail over allies. Demolishments appear to prevail over accomplishments. Non-successes appear to prevail over triumphs. Defeats appear to prevail over conquests. (&) Delinquencies appear to prevail over opportunities.

However, **I AM A MAN OF GOD**. And what exactly does that mean? It does not mean that I am bigger and better than anyone else. It does not mean that I deserve any form of special treatment. It does not mean that I do not face temptation. It does not mean that I do not experience problems or go through trials and tribulations.

But, it simply means that, as a born again Christian, *even though* and *when I do* go through problems, I am still going to have **something to live for**. We are all God's children – men and women of God, regardless of age. And it is significantly important that we stand strong, steadfast, and unmovable, with faith and hope, among this day in time, full of violence, problems and circumstances.

It is imperative that we recognize not only the worth but the moral and spiritual opportunity that we have as men and women of God. It is principal that we successfully stand on the Word of God and his promises. It is important that we mount our feet on the solid ground that love never fails and in the end all things can and will work together for the good to them that love God and are called according to his purpose.

I Belong To God: Staying On The Christian Path to Success was written as a guide, composed of tips to remember, guidelines to keep in mind, concepts to impart into you, and perceptions to be sustained in your heart with an effort to help you stay on a positive path to success.

Not success in just anything, but success in God. This book is first applicable to teenagers and youth.

First, those who want a written mentorship to get to where God wants you to be in your school, church, and community.

Second, those who are currently on a positive path and can use this book as a conduit for encouragement and route to leadership success.

This is applicable secondly to adults as a channel for stabilization on the path to success in God.

Regardless of age, this book can and will have an effective impact on your life. Through this book, you will have the opportunity to be encouraged that yes, life is hard, but it's not too hard that you can't take it. It's hard enough for you to learn from it and live past it – the things of this world and its circumstances. Even in those, you do not belong to them. You Belong to God!

Chapter 1:

The Simplicity and Power of Prayer

Aren't you so glad that God is a personal God? There is no other religion that has the type of communication with the upper being that they believe in with their god that we have with ours.

OUR GOD - He's simply **personal**. He's not private. He's very **public**. He's not hard-hearted. He's **compassionate**.

He has a heart that has never been understood and will never be understood by any man on earth or any angel in heaven. His love is beyond our understanding. His love *is powerful, genuine,* and *gratefully* appreciated by us, as Christians. I know I definitely appreciate it.

Since the beginning of time, God has never been distant or reserved. He's never been so detached or unsociable that we could not talk to him. God has provided us with a way of communicating with him and that is through a little something called prayer.

Prayer is communication with God. It is a conversation, a chat, a talk, discussion, dialogue, etc. Easy right?

Prayer is Communication with God.

It definitely is not a hard thing to do. It is quite frankly easier than tenser. **No matter who you are, what you may do, or where you may come from, you can pray.** Prayer is not subjective upon the pastor or the preacher, the mother or the deacon, or the Sunday school teacher or any person with the high title or position in the church.

PRAYER IS FOR EVERYBODY! Anybody can pray!

And honestly, there is such a simplicity that resides in prayer, for it definitely is not as hard as people to try to make it out to be or some people try to receive it to be.

Many people try to bring forth or establish a set way to pray to other people in their teaching, through which they are trying to follow them in what they are doing, in their spiritual habits. You want a prayer to be powerful, in order for it to bring about some sort of change.

So, **in order for it to be powerful, it has to be personable**. It's not personable if it comes from somebody else and not from you. If you're saying a prayer that you truly do not have a good understanding about, then that prayer is not for you. If you are reciting a prayer that somebody else has made for you but you're not really feeling it, that prayer is not for you. A prayer has to be personable, something coming from you as an individual

Now, there is nothing wrong with stationery prayers at all. We all have prayers that we say in a stationery form such as prior to us eating our food, we say grace.

When I was little we said "God is great and God is good. Let us Thank Him For Our Food. By Our Hands we all are fed. Give us Lord our daily bread. Amen." We even have stationery prayers for us being dismissed from church when the pastor may say "May the Lord watch between me and thee, while we're absent, one from another," as the benediction. But you should certainly know what that prayer is talking about.

    Thus, the BIG question is <u>HOW DO WE PRAY</u>?!
Jesus gave us a perfect example of how to pray. We know it today as "The Lord's Prayer."
And I'm going to break down the prayer for you – If you want, you can try to take some of these concepts that Jesus used in his prayers in yours as well:

1) **OUR FATHER WHO ART IN HEAVEN**
    By Jesus, starting out saying this right here alone, he established two things that quick: who we are and who God is. God is in heaven. We are on earth. When we pray, we should try to approach God, not in a completely soft manner, but still in a way where we are exemplifying that father-son/father-daughter type figure in thought and relationship in reality. He is our father. We should try to pray starting off recognizing who we are praying to, in whatever way that you feel comfortable.

2) **HALLOWED BE THY NAME**
    We must keep a balance in our communication with God. He's not our pal who we should talk to any kind of way. But, at the same time he is very close who we should feel comfortable talking to. Jesus said "hallowed by thy name". Hallowed means to be holy. Basically, Jesus is saying you are holy. That's what we have to remember. God is holy and he is different from us. We must sustain that knowledge of difference in our prayers to make sure that we are keeping respect at all times. That's the second thing that he established.

3) **THY KINGDOM COME, THY WILL BE DONE, ON EARTH AS IT IS IN HEAVEN**

This is basically the praise part right here. Because Jesus is saying You are the almighty God, Alpha and Omega, Beginning and End, First and Last, you are the king of your kingdom that we live in and dwell in on this earth. He's giving him the glory. He's giving him the honor. He is giving him the praise for who he is, not necessarily what for he has done. And lastly, he says, Let your will be done. Whatever you want to happen, let it happen. And however you want it to happen, let it happen that way. No matter how hard we may try, we must not forget that no matter how much we pray or plead unto God, if God has something set one way in his will, that's something that cannot change. We can change our destiny, but we cannot change his will. When we pray, we should keep that in mind, that God knows what he's doing and has it all under his control. Jesus basically says, However, way you have it up in heaven, God, let it be brought forth here on earth.

4) **GIVE US THIS DAY, OUR DAILY BREAD**

When we pray this part in the Lord's prayer, we are basically recognizing that we simply are grateful to be alive. We don't have to be alive. We could be dead, sleeping in our graves. God did not have to wake us up this morning, by any type of higher obligation. He is God. Therefore, anytime that we still have breath in our body we should be more than excited and willing to be thankful unto him and to bless his name. We are grateful to have an opportunity to be blessed with the things that we are blessed with because God is not obligated to do anything for us. God said that he would provide us with all of our needs. Notice, that the bible never said our wants, because sometimes our wants are not at all what we need. Gratefulness is the key.

5) **AND FORGIVE US OUR TRESPASSES, AS WE FORGIVE THOSE WHO TRESPASS AGAINST US**
Jesus is asking on our behalf for God to forgive us. That's one of the reasons why Jesus came down unto this earth, so that his blood would shed as a ransom for our sins. With that, one day, our sins would be forgiven. He's interceding on our behalf: Even though, we may not deserve it, please God forgive us.

6) **LEAD US NOT INTO TEMPTATION BUT DELIVER US FROM EVIL**
There is temptation all around us in the areas that we visit and the things that we do. There is always somebody or something that is out there to tempt us to do something that God has told us not to do. Sin is a large force, along with evil. So, Jesus is praying to help us God to avoid temptation and to stay out of it. And carry us out from evil. We should definitely include this in our prayers. It is a good thing for us to repent daily and ask God to keep us on the path that we need, that we may walk in the path of righteousness.

7) **FOR THINE IS THE KINGDOM, THE POWER, AND THE GLORY, FOREVER AND EVER, AMEN**
Whatever way that you start something, you want to try to finish it the same way. If you start a prayer strong, you should finish it just as strong. He starts out recognizing who God is and how powerful and different he is and ends doing the exact same thing.

The Lord's Prayer is simple and amazing. It's not too extravagant. It does not exaggerate. It is done in decency and in order, in a meek way. <u>But, it has great power.</u> It has concepts that can be admired and utilized in our daily and sporadic prayer.

Be sure to understand that your prayers do not have to be exactly the same as the Lord's prayer each time that you pray, however, it can always be used a positive reference point to denote to when approaching God.

Like I said before, prayer is what you make it to be. Whether you want it to be long or short is your choice. Whether you want it to include deep spiritual terms is your choice. The details of **YOUR** prayer are **YOUR** choice because it is YOURS!

> *The details of YOUR prayer are YOUR choice because it is YOURS!*
> **PRAY YOUR WAY**

<u>*Allow very few individuals to intercede into your prayer life.*</u>

Prayer is your straightforward communication with God and you do not want too many individuals interfering with your communication with the most high. Depending on many things, including the confidential qualities of you and the inner thoughts of the other individual, it can affect it positively and worse, negatively.

PRAYER HAS POWER AND AUTHORITY!
Here is why............

When Jesus died, he rose and got back up with all Power and Authority in his hands. He didn't leave it all to himself. He gave it all to us. Who is us?

Christians. Those who believe that he is their personal Savior and that he died on the cross for their sins, so that they may be forgiven, and working diligently towards living the life that he taught.

It was the advantage that Christians would have and the remaining advantage that we still have today. We now have power and we have authority.

INDIVIDUAL POWER! The church is a building that should live in you. With that being said, remember the single, solitary command that you have over your situations, by yourself. It is a great thing to have a Pastor or spiritual leader to call on when you need to get in contact with God; but, it is even a greater thing to distinguish the self-confidence in your prayers that, you alone have power in the things that you ask God for, by yourself.

There is power in unified prayers, as well; but you can get more personal with God when you are by yourself, on your knees, and praying – and one thing about God is that when you get personal with him, he will get personal with you. You have power.

Not only that, but you have Authority. Think about what you know about authority. You do not have successful authority if you are asking for the things that you desire. You do not have successful authority if you are begging for the things that you want done.

If you ever observe a president, ambassador, CEO, principal, manager, or any other type of person in authority, what makes them authoritative is when they take control. What makes them authoritative is that they don't ask for change, plead for it, request it, inquire it, probe it, but **COMMAND IT!**

When you command for something to happen, and all qualifications are deemed to be met, it shall be done.

Before Jesus died, yes, we still did have power. We had power to heal the sick. Moses had the power to part the red sea. David had the power to fight

Goliath. Joshua had the power to make the sun and the moon sit still. And the list continues. But, the power that we had was through a prayer without command.

Now that Jesus has died, he gave us **AUTHORITY** through our prayer that gives us POWER. This authority is accessed through two things. The first thing is faith. The bible gives the best definition of faith that I have ever seen.

Not one book, encyclopedia, website, or person, has given, in my opinion, a better definition of faith than in the book of Hebrew in the 11th chapter.

"<u>Faith is the substance of things hoped for and the evidence of things not seen</u>." It didn't say that faith is the substance of things hoped for and the evidence of things seen. But, it said the evidence of things not seen.

Faith is believing without having everything in front of you. It is seeking evidence without your eyes, but instead with your heart. Faith is trusting in what you are certain of without having all of the substantiation that finds what you believe in true beyond a shadow of a doubt.

<u>**As long as you believe with all of your heart, mind, and soul that Jesus Christ is your Lord and Savior, as you long as you have full confidence in who Jesus is and what he came to do, as long as you trust that he's coming back soon, if you believe that you've got power, then you have got the faith that you need**</u>.

You can't have a little bit of faith and expect for something to happen. You can't have a partial amount of faith and actually believe that change is getting ready to occur. It is only when you unleash your full potential faith that is inside of you for to beable to access your Christian Authority.

The second thing that is needed to access the authority given to us in order to receive power is a name.

A Name that is above every name. A name that you can call on and demons have to tremble. A name that you can call on and situations must turn around. A name that you can call on and those who are in the back will end up in the front. A name that you can call on and the atmosphere must change.

That name is JESUS! At the name of Jesus, every knee has got to bow and every tongue has got to confess that Jesus Christ is Lord to the glory of God the father. Jesus said to us that whatsoever we ask in his name we shall receive it.

Those are the two things that you must have in order to access your Christian authority to have earthly power to do spiritual things. **You need faith and the name of Jesus.**

When you pray, if you have faith larger than the size of a mustard seed without any sense of doubt and you close out with the name of Jesus, you ought to know that your prayer will have power. Therefore, I charge you to…..

Pray with command. After all, that's what Jesus died so that we could do. He died so we were not so vulnerable to the things that we encounter and the personal attacks from the enemy.

Pray to remove healing from our bodies. If you are sick in your body you can become well. Lay your hands over what is not well, and declare it healed.

Pray to raise the dead. This doesn't have to relate to the deceased in life. But, this can relate to the things that have died out in your life that once were alive. You can speak it to be flourishing in the name of Jesus.

Pray to reconcile financial needs. God created money and so he has control over it. You do not belong to quantities nor qualities of your wallet. You belong to virtues of your mind. Therefore, pray for God to show himself God in your wealth.

Pray to rebuild careers. God never closes a door without opening up another one. Now, that second door might take a long time to open up but you must believe that eventually, at some point, it will. Pray that the job you always wanted is yours and if it is the will of God, he will manifest your request.

Pray to rectify your family. A family that prays together stays together. That is more than just a saying; that is actually the truth. And even if you can't find it for your family to pray with you like you want, pray on your family's behalf because God will occupy your prayer and populate it amongst those who you pray for.

Pray to do anything that you need. There are no limits.

Don't underestimate the power of God.

Do not find the miracles and amazements in the bible to be some sort of fantasy, and distant from present need. God still is able to help us just like he helped them. We've got to have faith and believe that what we pray for it shall come to pass. We serve a God who is able to do exceedingly abundantly above all that we can ever ask or think.

Knowing that, that should be an assurance throughout the day that "If I pray, I've got a change coming in my life or in the life of somebody else."

Pray as you go throughout the day. Your eyes don't have to be closed to pray. Here's what I do:

> When I wake up in the morning, I get out of my bed, get down on my knees, and simply say "Thank you Jesus for another day." But instead of me saying Amen, I keep going throughout my day and as I see an ambulance or a fire truck driving by I pray saying "Bless them". If I pass by a high school, I say "Let them have a good day at school today." If someone calls me and lets me know of some distressing news, I pray about the situation. If I feel any sort of pain, I pray for that. If I pass by someone who is without a home or a place to stay, I pray that God will help them with what they need. And simply as I go throughout my day I variably am

having a conversation with God. That's what prayer is – and it's not so much that I am talking to God throughout the entire day and so every decision that I make is perfect or every step that I take is completely accurate, but it sure does make everything a lot better.

When I pray throughout the day, I simply have Jesus on my mind and so that way it makes it really hard for anything else nugatory to enter inside of it. If I have Jesus on the inside, I have something optimistic working on the outside. Another benefit that me praying throughout the day does is makes me spiritually feel safe on the inside. "If God is for me, who can be against me?" That scripture can effectively manifest in your life more when you can spiritually feel God working and living on the inside of you. That's how you feel when you're praying throughout the day. Additionally, another benefit is that it allows you to literally keep an automatic-mental prayer list. How many people tell you a day to pray for them? How many people tell you a day that they need prayer for themselves or somebody else and the things that they are going through? How many people do you say to them 'I'll pray for you'? Now, how often do you remember each and every person that tells you that? When you're praying throughout the day, as soon as someone tells you or talks to you about something like that, it is nearly impossible for you to forget them, because when they say it, you start praying right then, right there, in a hurry, at that moment.

PRAYER IS THAT POWERFUL! Whether on a group basis or on an individual basis, it is still powerful!

> **Whether on a group basis or on an individual basis, it is still powerful!**

The bible says that when two or three are gathered together in Jesus' name, God is in the midst.

What happens when God is in the midst? There is power. There is power to do anything that you need. Find you some prayer partners – people who have either been through some of the same things that you have been through or are going through some of the same things that you are going through - people who can relate to the same things and who can pray about the same things. Because when you ALL pray there will be a feeling that they will have that will cause a moral connection between you and them.

You can't really expect for people who have never been in your shoes to pray for exactly what you need because they do not know what you need.

They can pray in general on or around the topic. They can pray, asking that God will give you what you need to make it through whatever you're going through. But, the exact specifications for a prayer that is of your necessity, will unfortunately, never exist from another individual, if that individual has not experienced what you have experienced.

You should find people who can intercede on your behalf when talking to God, being able to say "God, help him/her with ____ (specifically, verbatim, explicitly)".

Establish people in your life who are going to be able to pray for you when you're going through – this way, when you're going through, you are also growing through.

And then don't forget! Pray for Yourself!

That is where you have the most power! Find yourself what the bible calls "a secret place" where it's just you and God. Find you a closet, a bathroom, a room nobody barely goes in, and let that be that special place of prayer, where you don't mind getting down on your knees and forgetting about what may be surrounding you or who may possibly hear you through the walls.

Seclude and isolate yourself from any distractions, anybody, or anything who will be a hindrance in your interaction with God. Get personal and actually pour your heart out to the Lord that you need his help.

The truth is that we are living in a day in time, when prayer is not only becoming an asset, but it has become a necessity, especially upon us, as Christians. It will bring about any type of spiritual and earthly assistance that we desire. We've got everything that we need in order to be a powerful people when it comes to prayer. The opportunity is within you! Even as youth, young men and women of God, God can use you, but we've got to be willing to talk to him first.

Chapter 2:
I Don't Mind Waiting On The Lord

It has been stated that the hardest thing for man to do is wait; and I totally agree.

Some say it takes too long. Some say you might miss out on what you're waiting for. Some say in the process of waiting, you could grow to become weak. But, I do not think that that is the case.

It's all about what we are waiting for.

Often times when we are waiting on change, we wait on certain things in particular to change. If and when we do this, we unfortunately grow weary and sometimes weak.

We become discouraged and sometimes feel down. We become ill of our problems and sometimes dispirited. And so, to avoid all of this, instead of waiting on certain things to change, we must, instead, learn how to otherwise wait on the Lord. ***Because when you wait on God, everything else you need comes along with it.***

It takes patience. Patience is the ability to wait. In life period, we have to learn how to wait. Waiting is a necessary component of life. Not everything comes quick, fast, in a hurry, right at that moment in every situation. No matter who you are, time does not speed up for anybody. So, it's important to wait #1 to achieve any goal, #2 to overcome any obstacle #3 to become wiser and simply better.

> *It's Important to Wait...*
> #1 to achieve any goal
> #2 to overcome any obstacle
> #3 to become wiser and simply better.

A man who waits gets his reward in due time and not only that but grows his or her character. We must wait on some of the things of this world to *grow wiser realistically.* That same way, we must wait on God and the things of God to *grow wiser spiritually.*

There is a necessity for us to have an equal balance in the things that we wait on and for in life. So, by knowing how important waiting on God is and how it can grow you spiritually, there is a necessity that now, more than ever, with everything going on in the world today, that we develop a mindset when we are honestly, willing and able to say "I Don't Mind Waiting On The Lord."

Wherever you are reading this book, if there's somebody there near you, look at them and say "I Don't Mind Waiting On The Lord."

How you can really say that with faith and belief, is with the right perspective. The major concern in waiting, regardless of what the situation may be, is What Happens During Waiting? I will be honest and will not tell a lie.

You may experience hurt, as well as pain. Friends may leave you and when it comes to what you're waiting for or on, family may not believe you. Trials and tribulations will be experienced. Difficulties will be brought before you. I can name so many but many of you who have been waiting for a while already know. The biggest thing is how to get through it.

So, I put together an acronym that I want you to remember – P.I.A. <u>P.I. A. stands for Pray, Ignore, Anticipate.</u>

We're going to take a quick minute in this chapter and briefly discuss each one:

P – Pray
I – Ignore
A - Anticipate

1st Pray. Praying, as we talked about in the first chapter, is not nearly as difficult as it is sometimes made out to be.

Prayer is simply communication with God. And since that's the case, it is very much possible to pray without ceasing. Best believe that your eyes don't have to be closed in order to pray.

You can pray as you talk. You can pray as you walk. You can pray as you do things throughout the day. As long as you finish off that prayer, like I told you, at the end of the night, before you go to bed with Through Jesus Name I Pray Amen, everything is alright. With so many reasons, there are so many opportunities.

This may sound weird but *prayer will help you feel better*. **The more you pray and call on Jesus, the better you will feel.**

2nd is ignore. Ignore the people who don't like you. Ignore the people who are against you. According to the Encarta World Dictionary, the word ignore means to refuse to notice or pay attention to somebody or something.

You can listen to somebody or something, and in some cases, you have to, but you do not have to pay attention to them.

Thus, People that try to tell you that your waiting is not worth it – ignore them. People who don't believe in the opportunities put in front of you – ignore them. People who see more doubts than ways out in your situation – ignore them.

<u>Ignore! Ignore! Ignore!</u> Don't let those type of people get into your head, because eventually it will cause you to start thinking like them – and that is probably one of the worse situations to be in; to actually start to think the things your haters and enemies call you or accuse you of being or doing. The biggest and greatest way to avoid that is by ignoring them.

3rd is anticipate. It's one thing to wait. But you've got to wait with anticipation. Know for yourself what you are waiting on. Don't lose faith. Hang on in there. Anticipate what God has in store for you after your waiting is over. Hold on to God's Promise. You Can Do It! How Do I know it? Because there were several people in the bible who waited on the Lord as well.

Let me give you some examples

First, let's look at **Noah**. Noah was told by God to build an ark of gopher wood because God was going to flood the earth. He gave Noah several specifications that led him to detailed particulars on how he wanted it done. Noah built the ark and waited for years to see the earth flooded. But, he waited.

Abraham! Abraham waited for God to bless him and his wife Sarah with a child and waited for a long time. But, they waited.

Moses! After turning water into blood, and causing plagues involving frogs, flies, and fire and so forth, Moses waited on Pharaoh to let God's people go. But, he waited.

Job! Job was a man who God offered to Satan to tempt. For 30 something years, Job was sick in his body. He lost everything that he had; his family, friends, his job, his material wealth – EVERYTHING! But, he waited.

Oh and let's not forget about **JESUS**! We can't forget about him. When they put the crown of thorns onto his head, he had to wait on God. When they made him carry his own cross up that hill called Calvary, he had to wait on God. When they put nails in his hands and nails in his feet in order to be able to attach his body onto the cross, he still had to wait on God. When he was laying on the cross and said his last, final words, he was still waiting on God; but not for long because all of that was one day and only a few days to come, Jesus got up with all power in his hands. And look at him now.

He has a name that's above every name that At the Name of Jesus every knee has got to bow and every tongue has got to confess that Jesus Christ is Lord to the glory of God the father. Jesus waited on the Lord.

Now, after he suffered in his waiting, after HE struggled in his waiting, HE'S got the victory. We can wait on God too, because after WE struggle in our waiting, WE TOO will get the victory in our right hand so that we can have our testimony in our left.

Waiting on God has benefits that this world just can't give you.

> **Waiting on God has benefits that this world just can't give you.**

My thing is this → We wait on the things of this world, tell me why can't we wait on the Lord. ←(Good question to ask yourself)

When we go to the doctor's office to get a procedure done or just to get a checkup or to see a loved one, we have to wait in the waiting room. If we can wait on the doctor in the waiting room, why is it that we cannot wait on the Lord?

When it's the first or half way in the month and it's time to get paid, we wait for our check to come in the mail or for our direct deposit to be processed into our account. If we can wait for some money, why is that we cannot wait on the Lord?

When somebody or something comes to town that we really wanna see and we go to their concert or production, we have to wait in line to get in or even better yet, wait for the thing to start. If we can wait in line for a concert, If we can wait in line for a production to start, why is it that we cannot wait on the Lord?

When we're at a football or basketball game, we have to wait for it to begin. If we can wait for a football or basketball game, why is it that we cannot wait on the Lord?

When we go to an amusement park, we have to wait in line for our turn to ride a ride. If we can wait to ride a ride or see something at Six Flags, Disney World, White Waters, Lake Winnipesaukee, Zoo Atlanta, the Georgia Aquarium, Bush Gardens or Universal Studios, please tell me why is it that we cannot wait on the Lord.

When we go to the Post Office to mail something off, we have to wait in that long line. If we can wait in line at the Post Office, why is it that we cannot wait on the Lord?

When we're on our phones or on the internet on YouTube, we have to wait on the video to buffer so we can watch it. If we can wait for 15 minutes for a video to pop up on YouTube, tell me why is it that we cannot wait On the Lord?

When we're in traffic, we stop, then go, then stop, then go, and stop, then go, and stop, then go. If we can wait on the traffic to pass by or if we can go through traffic, surely we can wait on the Lord.

When we see a DVD commercial, we have to wait on our favorite movie to come out on DVD. If we can wait on our favorite movie to come out on DVD or On Demand, surely brothers and sisters we can wait on the Lord.

Waiting on the things of this world is one thing. Waiting on the things of this world to change is one thing. But, waiting on God is something totally different. Because they that wait upon the Lord......... God is greater than every enemy! God is greater than every problem! And the greatness of our God allows our *after-shock* to be even more powerful!

Some of you today reading this book have so many problems on every hand. Some of you today have situations that simply cannot be named. But, I dare you after you get finished reading this chapter to wait on the Lord. Wait On Him! Wait On Him!

Chapter 3:
Standing Out > Fitting In

If you are a young person or a teenager → definitely pay attention to this chapter.

At the age of 3, my mother and father enrolled me into Greenforest/McCalep Christian Academic Center in Decatur, Georgia. My first teacher was Mrs. Carter, who I thank until this day because, believe it or not, I had a speech impediment that hindered my speech and the enunciation of my words. You definitely couldn't tell now because I talk a lot all throughout the day and fluently at that. I attended the Early Learning Center until the age of 4 when I graduated from Pre-K.

It was then that I went on to the "big school". I remained a student at Greenforest until the 5th grade and loved every bit of it. It was an amazing school. It was a Christian Academy, therefore, I was able to freely do one of the things that I love to do most, praise the Lord.

Nobody stopped me. In fact, other students would join me because they believed in the same thing that I believed in and we all had a passion for God; a true passion – to the point that we could praise God all day, listen to gospel music all day and none of us would get tired of it.

We would put on programs on Grandparents Day, Founders Day, Easter, and one of our favorites was Christmas. I joined the chorus in 4th and 5th grade. And one of the things that I thoroughly enjoyed the most was chapel.

Chapel was held on every Monday and Wednesday. It lasted for about an hour and was basically church because we had the opportunity to praise and worship God. Sometimes we even had a speaker or a preacher who would come and bring forth the word of God.

There were reenactments of bible stories and the list continues. There were so many great things about Greenforest that I admired and loved about the school but the main thing that I enjoyed was the fact that my spirituality was \ allowed to mix and intersperse with my education.

I left Greenforest in the 5th grade. My parents entered me into DeKalb County Schools at Champion Theme Middle School in Stone Mountain, GA. I was very excited about attending Champion because I heard so many great things and it would be my first time being a part of a public school, considering that I had been in a private school setting for nearly all of my life until that point.

Eventually, I started to become anxious and panicky and tense to what exactly it was that I should expect. I knew that it would be different and it would be a totally different experience, especially since I was going directly into middle school and was not making a transition within a certain level of school. But, uniquely, I never was scared.

There was not at one point that I was frightened or terrified about what it was that I would get into. I was instead eager and enthusiastic about the experiences that were yet to come. I was determined of my character and how, no matter what other characters may come my way, I refused to allow that to change mine.

Easier than what I expected, I adapted to Champion very well.

There was a difference. There was no freely expressing of religion. I couldn't go around singing in the hallways, or humming gospel songs in classrooms. I couldn't pray with students in public anymore. There were no more teachers reading us bible stories at the beginning of the day and having bible study. So, it was different.

Above all, the main thing that was different was the students and the new environment that I was surrounded by. A lot of the things that I saw in public school were totally foreign to me because my friends at Greenforest did not do half of the things that they were doing in public school.

They were totally unalike and therefore, it took a lot of getting used to. But, before I went to Champion, my mother, father, family, and close friends told me, on a consistent basis, remain my image and not to allow anything to change who I am and what I stand for. I held strong to that.

Within the first couple of months of attending Champion, I was known by most of the kids in the school, sixth through eighth grade. For many of them, I preached at their church in the past or they've seen me on YouTube because by that time I was a "YouTube sensation." And what really escalated my "reputation" was in the first few months of me attending the school, the news aired an enormous story on me that aired all over Georgia and was advertised on the radio and so forth. It grew so far that so many thousands watched it. People knew who I was.

Exceptionally, A lot of people thought that would bring pressure but uniquely it didn't. It brought reassurance that what I was doing was for the right reason because I had individuals who were looking up to me as a role model that God can use them just as God has used me.

As I went throughout my three years at that school, I sustained an optimistic image, a noble man of God to be the best of my ability. That doesn't mean that I was perfect and never made a B on an assignment instead of an A but I tried my best to make sure that I stood my ground of who I was because I knew already that I am who God says that I am.

Everyone has transitions to make in life. Toddlers have the transition to make from Pre-school to Kindergarten. Youth have the transition to make from elementary school to middle school. Teens have the transition to make from middle school to high school. Young Adults have the transition from high school to college. Adults have the transition to make from education to career. The mature have the transition to make from career to retirement......and the list continues. There are transitions in all of our lives.

In my transition, I had two choices: **either to fit in** or **to stand out**. But, with both, there were consequences. This is the thought process that we need to keep in mind when we are trying to figure out what our stand within the transitions that we must make in life are.

Consequences of Fitting In

-Bad Habits
-Decisions Go Wrong
-Individuality Vanished
NEGATIVE

Consequences of Standing Out

-Identity Sustained
-Decisions Pay Off
-Positive Future
POSITIVE

Look at the difference – one is positive and one is negative. One will lead you onto a path of remorse, while the other will lead you onto a path of contentment. You will find yourself in a far better situation if you are caught standing out than fitting in.

Fitting in is all about being the same.

While……
Standing out is all about being *different*.

You should never grow up as a child, experience as a teenager, sentient as a young adult, or live as an adult trying to be the same as somebody else.

You are your person! You are special! You are different! And God made you that way for a reason! There is no fun in trying to be the same as somebody else and even deeper there is no legacy in that; because nobody will have anything special or unique or distinct to remember about who you were and what you stood for. Their memory of you would literally be the same another individual.

When you try to fit in, that's what happens. You literally try to find out how you can (1) be accepted and (2) experience the same thing that another person is experiencing.

THERE IS ABSOLUTELY NOTHING WRONG WITH BEING DIFFERENT!

It is you being different that allows you to be an individual. It is when you are common and the same that you become a cluster of a crowd; and that is not what you want to live by. You want to live with uniqueness and differentiality.

You want to be able to know and say for yourself "I'm Different!" We must not down each other for being different because being different is not a bad thing. Different does not mean despise or divide. But, different means unique and unite.

Different = Unique, Unite

Aim to establish your own unique characteristics that will help you grow into your own individualistic figure. That is what people will remember you by, being an individual who stood for something greater than your surroundings, greater than your odds, greater than your proposed opportunities by others.

It is having an individualistic figure that gives you the opportunity to be the change that you want to be in your life and the life of somebody else. It was because those inventors, civil rights activists, and idealists, recognized that they were different and an individual that they were able to bring forth some of the greatest opportunities that we have today.

Dr. Martin Luther King, Jr. would not have been able to turn this world upside down if he had not understood and accepted that fact that he was plain out different from everybody else.

In order for us to be able to get along with one another, under one accord, we must understand that we are all different. Therefore, when you see somebody or come across somebody who may be different from who you are, that's your opportunity to grasp on to their friendship to grow some of their characteristics inside of you.

That is what makes you an individual. Be different even when people try to tell you that you are abnormal, just because you may do something a little different from the normal way.

STAND OUT!

When you stand out against the things of this world, God will shine on the inside of you.

Wouldn't it be so amazing if you could walk into a room and people are able to know that you are a man or woman of God? Wouldn't it be so amazing if there could be hundreds of people in a room wearing the same clothes and out of everyone, you look different because people can see the Jesus that shines in you? That's how you want to be.

Standing out is much greater than fitting in.

<u>A Message to Youth</u>

I charge you wherever you go to stand out instead of fitting in. I charge you to go to school and to show that you are different because there is nothing wrong about. Allow your individuality to promote your grades, your involvement in extracurricular activities, a positive attitude and behavior, and a positive life in your home and community.

Chapter 4:
When There's Nothing Left But God, That's All You Need

God said in his Word that he would provide us with all of our needs according to his riches and his glory. Often times, when we think of this statement, we immediately think of what our bodies need, such as food and water.

Those who are doubters of the religion of Christianity and what we believe in, use that as a conduit to their message, but what they forget is the noteworthy statement that Jesus made when he was tempted by Satan. He said that man cannot live by just bread alone.

In other words, food, water, + other physical necessities will not fulfill our need to survive. Science may prove otherwise but the Word of God is a standpoint of proof that what I am stating is true. There is something else that is missing in the equation. That missing something is GOD.

Trust me, I know that science has provided evidence that there is a necessity for us to drink water and have fluids entering and exiting our body in order for us to survive as a species. I know that that same principle applies to food. I know that there are supposedly other physical necessities that rest as essentials for us to be able to survive.

But, just like God created us, he created science too. Henceforth, he still is God.

Nothing else or nobody else woke us up this morning but God. Nothing else or nobody else clothed us in our right mind but God. Nothing else or nobody else breathed life into our bodies, but God. Nothing else or nobody else allowed us to see, live, and experience another day but God.

So, when you really look at our living situation from a spiritual perspective, we recognize that we cannot live without God. God is the source of our strength and the strength of our life. Without him, we simply cannot live.

With that being said, when we are in situations when our faith is standing trial, and our friends leave us…..when we our family abandons us…..when people treat us wrong……when we've lost everything that we have ever had…..and we are simply in a dry state in our life and it seems as if there is nothing left, a question that is commonly asked is how still is God holding on to his promise that he would provide us with everything that we need? I'll tell you how – **we've still got him.**

We must not demote the opportunistic possibilities and greatness of simply having him. As long as God is in the picture, we've got everything that we need to survive. And we know that that stands forever because God will never leave us nor will he forsake us.

God is everything that we need and more, even when we don't have what we physically or morally think we need. God's got it all under control. He's got it all in his hands.

We can trust in God because we know that he is a Jehovah of many names and callings……

- **Jehovah-Bara** - *Lord Creator* - **Isaiah 40:28**

    He created the birds of the air and the creatures of the sea. He created the animals. He created the mountains and valleys, the trees, the rivers. When we look around and see the fascinations of this earth, it was God – his hands made it. Then, He created us with one simple breath that gave us the life that we live today. And even in God creating joy and peace, he also, sometimes, creates trials and tribulations for us to go through and experience. If God created trials and tribulations, he can bring us out of it as well.

- **Jehovah-Chatsahi** - *Lord my Strength* - **Psalm 27:1**

    Our strength is not found in anything or anyone else but the Lord. It is during our time of total darkness and despair, misery and desolation, hopelessness and anguish, feebleness and weakness, that there is a true necessity for us to depend on God the most in order for him to give us strength. We cannot handle the things that we go through on our own: trials and tribulations, as well as enemies have much power to do great things in our life that only God can give us strength to deal with. But, that's exactly why is there because when we are weak, God is strong. That's why we should lean on him in our time of disadvantage.

- **Jehovah-Chereb** - *Lord the Sword* - **Deut. 33:29**

    I know we've got guns now, which is probably one of the greatest individual weapons in the world's eyes. But, a gun, a knife, or anything of that, is nothing compared to God. As soldiers in the army of the Lord, we have the greatest weapon in our possession that outweighs all earthly weapons. This weapon is God. Look at David in the bible: David did not have any reasonable weapon that, when thought of earthly, could have in any way allowed him to be prosperous or victorious in his battle; but it wasn't so much of any fact that his strategy was so well. It was not so much of any fact that he was physically prepared to face what he had the face. But, it was all of the fact, that he had God. That was his weapon. That was his defense. God will show up and show out in your situation when you use him.

- **Jehovah-Gador Milchamah -** *Mighty in Battle* **- Ps 24:8**

    Yolanda Adams said that the battle is not yours, it is the Lords. It is so amazing how true that is. We do not need to fight our battles. As you know, God will set us up in battles, but he never loses control. God has his battles so much under control that he will fight them on our behalf. All we have to do is turn our battles and our problems over to the Lord and best believe he will work it out. We just must have faith and trust in him.

- **Jehovah-Ganan -** *Lord Our Defense* **- Ps 89:18**

    When the enemy comes in like a flood, the spirit of the Lord will create a standard against it. Danger is all around as we walk and as we talk. It surrounds us as we act and react. Danger is a large force along with evil in this world and there is absolutely no doubt that if we are not ready and are not equipped at all times, we will find ourselves in a situation that we cannot get out of. How do you stay equipped and ready? Through God. Whenever we have anything coming at us, whether it's a problem or an enemy, God is Lord Our Defense and will protect us from dangers seen and unseen.

- **Jehovah-Hamelech -** *Lord King* **- Psalm 98:6**

    He is the only God. No other God is before him in power, authority, and ability. You cannot get any higher than God. God is the King of Kings and the Lord of Lords. He sees all and controls all. So, if God sees all, and knows all, controls all, masters all, why not trust him in all situations!

- **Jehovah-Hashopet** - *Lord My Judge* - Judges 11:27

  It is not the job of a Christian to judge another Christian, nor is it the job of a Christian to judge one who is not a Christian. Not only is not our job, but it also is not our right. Who are we to judge anyone else? We were not saved all of our lives. There was a point in all of our lives, when we had to accept Jesus Christ as our personal savior, therefore, in that, we are saved. We do not have the right to judge one another because all of us have sinned and fallen short of the glory of God. The only person that has the right to judge us is God himself. Jehovah Hashopet

- **Jehovah-Jireh** - *Provider* - Gen. 22:14, I John 4:9, Philip 4:19

  God will provide us with everything that we need. That's the type of God that he is. He has not changed in that. David said "I have been young and now am old, yet never have I seen the righteous forsaken or his seed begging for bread." Whatever it is that we need, my God will supply. He can handle any must, any demand.

- **Jehovah-Machsi** - *Lord my Refuge* - Psalm 91:9

  In the time of trouble, in the time of despair, God will be your refuge. He will be your protection. He will be your asylum. He will be your retreat. He will be your safe haven, where you can go to when you need him the most. He's your hiding spot.

- **Jehovah-Mephalti** - *Lord my Deliverer* - Psalm 18:2

  If you're stuck in a situation that seems that there is no way out, God will be right there to make a way out of no way. He will deliver you out of the worse situations. There is nothing too hard for God.

- **Jehovah-Naheh** - *Lord who Smites* - Ezekiel 7:9

  It's not my job to try to punish or disrespect my enemies. If God is for me, who can be against me? When my enemies act against me, God will discipline them the way that he feels necessary.

- **Jehovah-Rohi** - *Shepherd* - Psalm 23

  God is the ultimate shepherd. He will take care of his flock. He will not allow anything that he doesn't want to happen to you happen to you. He's got you protected and safe in his arms. Those who act against you, he will take care of them. David said "He will prepare a table before you in the presence of your enemies."

- **Jehovah-Rophe** - *Healer* - Isaiah 53:4,5

  God is a healing God. There is no sickness that God does not have the capability of healing. When the doctors have given up on you, and you have lost faith in your opportunities, regardless of what the sickness may be, God can and will heal your body. He'll make you strong. He'll help you hold out just a little while longer. God will make you whole.

- **Jehovah-Sel'i** - *Lord my Rock* - Psalm 18:2

  An old songwriter once said "Where Do I Go when I don't have someone to turn to? Who Do I talk to when nobody wants to listen? And who do I lean on when there's no foundation stable? I can Go to the Rock, I know he's able. I can Go to the Rock."

- **Jehovah-Shalom** - *Peace* - Isaiah 9:6, Rom 8:31-35

God will give you everlasting peace in the time of a storm – that type of peace that surpasses all understanding and earthly knowledge. Experiencing the total peace of God is a wonder and an amazing experience.

- **Jehovah-Shammah -** *Present* **- Hebrews 13:5**

We serve an Omnipresent God. He can be here, there, and everywhere at the same time. Just when we think he is not present, he's with us at all times.

JEHOVAH!

And there's more!

As you see, God is everything that you need and more. So, whenever you find yourself in a situation when you're stuck between a rock and a hard place, just remember "JEHOVAH".

Jehovah will keep you in the valley. Jehovah will heal your every sickness even when the doctors have given up on you. Jehovah will deliver you from a financial situation, even when you don't have any money left to your name. Jehovah will be food to eat. Jehovah will be your water to drink.

Jehovah will be there with you until the very end. Jehovah will turn your stumbling into stepping stones. Jehovah will turn your present into the past. Jehovah will guide you through the difficulties of life. Jehovah will hide you from the rain in a difficult storm.

Jehovah will forgive you of your sins. Jehovah will comfort you in the midst of distress. Jehovah will be everything and give you everything that you need. JEHOVAH!

Hopefully, that will pop in your mind - who God is compared to our needs. When there is nothing left but God, that's all you need!

Chapter 5:

Putting God First

As many of you may already know, God has established a will in all of our lives. He has our life planned out before we are placed in our mother's womb.

God already knows who we are, what we are going to do, and how we are going to do it. He knew that you were going to read this book at this exact time and at this exact place. He knows our weaknesses and our strengths, our failures, the trials and tribulations that we're going to have to go through and even the goals that we are going to end up accomplishing.

In summation, I state that God knows what our life is destined to be. Theologically, we know him to be *omnificent* because *he is all-knowing*. We must realize that, because his will has upon plan in our life, there is absolutely nothing that our God does not know about us.

The grand fact is "He Knows It All." He's got it all in his hands. God is known as the All in All for a reason.

And so, think about it this way: If God is our all in all, he sees all, conducts all, and knows all, why would we not put our ALL into him. Further thought about, if you put YOUR all into THE ALL, your ALL becomes the BEST!

From the moment that we are born, as we live, even in the early adolescence of life, we develop dreams and aspirations of who we want to be and what we want to do. The common occupations of many little kids who have dreams of what they want to be are doctors, lawyers, teachers, preachers, and the list continues.

In those dreams and aspirations, we simply want to be successful and be the best at what we do. Success is the goal. The big question is what is the key to being successful? What concept mandates success in our goals? What Is the ultimate key that will land as a standpoint to and for success.

Stating in complete honesty, If we were to try to answer that question with specifics, our responses would number tremendously to things such as watch your friends, never give up, don't pay attention to enemies or haters, stay on the path to education, stay encouraged, say no to the things that are not right, remain strong and determined to the things that you believe in and more. Those are tips.

In other words, those are suggestions. What does that mean? It means, yes, they have worked for other people in the past and people right now, in their situation, but just because one thing works for one person, that does not mean that that same thing will work for another.

That is why the path to success differs for different people. Everybody's situations of the components of their life are all different. In this chapter, I want to present to you the ultimate key to success in anything that you do.

This is not a concept, tip, or suggestion. It is the key that, literally, in all cases, ensures success, as an individual. This key is: **PUTTING GOD FIRST!**

There is no such thing as a failure, when God is put first. Things are taken care of the way that God wants you to, in a unique manner when God is put first.

Simply, nothing can go wrong, even when it seems like it at times, when God is put first. When God is put first, if an obstacle comes up to you as an encounter, your spirit speaks first before your mind. In other words, your spirit has a mind of its own.

> When God is put first, if an obstacle comes up to you as an encounter, your spirit has a mind of its own.

Therefore, YOU don't act but the HOLY SPIRIT is acting for you and you don't even know it! Isn't that amazing? The entire fact that putting God first can take you so far. It is a spiritual investment that never comes back void. It always returns valid among all situations.

> **God – 1st**
> **Family - 2nd**
> **Work – 3rd**

I know you've probably all heard the classification of our priorities, which is "God first, Family second, work third."

God is supposed to be first. Putting God first indicates what God said when he gave his first commandment, which was You shall have no other gods before me and reinforces what Matthew said, which was "Seek ye first the kingdom of God…".

God is a jealous God. He wants the glory, honor, and the praise. And with that comes reward. Therefore, when you recognize God in heaven, he will praise you on earth.

So, when you invite God and put him first in every single area of your life, those areas become blessed. Think harder into what God said in his first commandment among the ten *"You shall not have any gods before me"*.

When God stated this, he was not only talking about spiritual Gods but sometimes we put faith in some of the things of this world, when we should not.

Sometimes we put faith in money. Sometimes we put faith in people. Sometimes we put faith in material things. And the spirituality of the matter is that anytime we put our faith in anything else but God, they become a god in our life. God wants to be put first.

He wants all of our faith to be put in him. We can believe in certain things. We can trust certain things. But, we should only have faith in one thing and that is God.

There is no doubt, that as Christians, living in a hard day in time, it is very hard putting God first. There are several reasons why putting God first is extremely hard sometimes.

First and foremost, God is a God that we cannot physically see with our corporeal eye; and so, it takes faith to believe and act in the words that he has established upon this earth. Otherwise, opposed to us not being able to physically see God, we can physically see the things that lure us in the most and the other things that we have the opportunity to put first.

The world looks like it can offer everything: pleasure, entertainment, education, socialization, and more. But, GOD can offer ETERNAL LIFE. And I'll tell you when it's all said and done, and your life here on earth is done and over, it's not about all that the world had to offer you, it's not about all of earthly things that you could intake, it's all about the spiritual things that you could intake, and how well enough you put got first before everything else.

I don't know about you but I want to go to heaven and it's a narrow strait getting there, but I'm willing to live the best life I can here on earth so I can manifest an even better one in heaven.

The reason why I can have this mindset is not because life is just so easy and laid-back, but because I know who stands for me, and it's more than the world that stands against me.

Greater is he that is in me than he that is the world. If God is for me, who can be against me? And as long as I put him first, he will make sure that I'm going in the right path I need to be on in order to gain his positive status. That's the attitude we have to possess.

Don't look to other people for answers before you have come to God. The best way to keep God first is to Pray before you do anything.

Like I said before, your eyes don't have to be closed in order to pray. Pray throughout the day as you carry out your normal day to day duties. Pray. Don't wait until something goes wrong or is getting ready to go wrong and there is nothing else for us earthly to do and then turn to God and pray.

Pray even when you don't have anything to ask God. Pray simply because you feel like it. And then when you pray, be willing to wait for his answers. Even if it takes a long time, wait on the Lord. Don't give him a deadline as soon as you start praying. You can't pray effectively when you've given God a deadline for how long you're going to give him to do what you want him to do in your life, in your situation.

We've got to remember that God's time is not like our time. Peter said that with the Lord, a day is like a thousand years, and a thousand years is like a day.

The second best way to put God first is OBEDIENCE. Obedience will take you so far when it comes to God. We all know that God works in mysterious ways. He doesn't tell us everything and when he might tell us to do something it may not, in our minds, make the most sense at the beginning, but in order for it to make the most sense in the end, you've got to just do what he tells you to do.

Obedience is nothing far from complying to somebody's authority. If God said it, you can't change it, rearrange it, and so, God said it, believe it, do it, and act in it. We can't question God's methods for he's God and he knows what he's doing. He created our problems and because of that, he can help us get through them much better than we can.

Put God first. He will lead you in the right direction. He will lead you to where he wants you to be. He will help you get through the things of life because the reality of the matter is that no matter well your strategy may be, you cannot get through them on your own.

Chapter 6:
There Is A Destiny Behind Your Experiences

Have you ever read the book of Job?

I love that book in the bible. And if you have not read it, whenever you get the chance, create a schedule/plan for you to read it as soon as possible. It will inspire you. The entire book surrounds this one man by the name of Job.

Job resembles some of us today that go through things, insofar as some of his concepts are concerned.

Job was an upright man. He was a good person but all of sudden detrimental things started to happen to him. Problems were just arising on ever hand. He had some of the worse experiences.

For one, he was personally attacked by the devil. And sometimes he did lose his temper and got mad. Sometimes he did feel down and out. There were several times when he did feel a little discouraged. But, never did he lose faith in his deliverance. He consistently believed that if God brought him to it, he will surely bring him out of it.

Let's talk about the story. Job was perfect and upright. He feared God. Additionally, he Eschewed, which in other words means shunned or avoided, evil. He was very genealogically blessed as God had blessed him with *7 sons* and *3 daughters*. Then he was materialistically blessed because he had *7,000 sheep, 3,000 camels, 500 yoke of oxen* and *500 donkeys*.

Plus he had a great household. He kept everything in order. One thing that he did was: after his sons and daughters would feast and have their parties, he would offer up a burnt offering to God because he felt as if they had sinned. And the list continues.

Overall, this man had it all under control. He was the closest to perfect that you could get and he was blessed with so much land and so much cattle and such a great household.

So, Satan comes up to heaven to talk to God. God says Where did you come from? (Not like God didn't know or anything like that)

Satan responds and says you know just doing my thing walking and roaming the earth, seeing what's going on, terrorizing people's lives and tempting people to turn against you. Let me tell you: Satan felt a little accomplished. He basically tried to told God off.

God got back at him and said well have you considered my servant Job? There's no one on earth like him. He's this….. He's that……. You should try to tempt him and see what you get out of him. Satan was not expecting that. But, God knew exactly what he was doing and he had full confidence in what Job was going to do.

Notice brothers and sisters, God offered Job. Satan didn't ask about Job. But, God offered him. Sometimes God will offer you to be tempted. That should let you know that you're special. But, here's the reality, like I said before, God won't bring you to it, if he won't bring you out of it.

> **God won't bring you to it, if he won't bring you out of it.**

His word still lives today when it said in 1 Corinthians 10:13 that he will not suffer you to be tempted above that ye are able. He will never put more on you than you can bear.

Well Satan says well he's blessed. He's got a nice house. Nice land. A lot cattle. A lot of children.

He said – "he only loves you for what you do for him, not for who you are. So, I guarantee you God if all of what he has is taken away, he will stop being oh so faithful to you and find you an enemy than a friend, in fact I promise you he will curse you right in your face."

God said that's where you got it wrong. But, you can prove your own self wrong. So, he said you can do whatever you want to do. But, you cannot touch him. In other words tempt him but don't kill him.

Let me stop right there for a second. Let's talk about the difference between the power of God and the power of Satan.

With God, there is no extent. With Satan, there is. God is Omni present, meaning that he can be in multiple places at one time. Satan is solo-present, meaning that he can only be at one place at one time.

There is a limit to where Satan can go and there is a limit to what Satan can do. He has regular angelic power just like the angels in heaven and just like them, they don't even have all of the power.

God is the almighty. He is the one that has all of the power. So, here is the deal. If Satan does not have God's support, he cannot do it. God permits Satan to tempt us; not to terminate us but to strengthen us - to make us stronger. But, when God allows Satan to tempt us, he only gives him so much power that he can work with, and gives him certain limitations, as well, that he has.

So, let's get back to the story. God said Alright. You can touch his surroundings but don't touch him. In other words don't kill him.

In 1 day this is what happened: (It was a dramatic experience for Job) First the Sabeans came and attacked his servants and took all the oxen and donkeys.

Then, fire from heaven came down to burn his sheep and his servants.

Next, the Chaldeans swept down his camels and later all of his 7 sons and 3 daughters were killed. He was told of these things happening to him back to back. I cannot imagine how Job must have felt. I'm sure he probably wondered:

Why is all of this happening to good old me – especially when I am doing the will of God? Why is all of this happening to me, especially when I am being as obedient as I possibly can and trying my best to live as God desires? It was a compilation of a whole bunch of things happening back to back.

It was unreal. It was entirely abnormal. It was because the devil personally attacked Job.

Do you ever wonder why some of the things that we go through in our lives just seem to be real sometimes, like you're the only person in life who would ever endure some of the things that we are going through?

Some of us, like Job, wonder how some of the things that we experience even happen. Sometimes it's the devil actually attacking you. But, here's the comfort in knowing this, you must have something about you or within that other people just don't have.

Like I said the devil is solo-present. He can't be everywhere at the same time. He can only be at one place at one time. He's not unwise or thoughtless. He's very smart and so he uses his time wisely and makes intelligent decisions. He does not waste his time. He will not waste his time on somebody that doesn't have anything that he can use. He won't waste his time on somebody that doesn't have any faith in God. He only tests God's most noble believers. So you ought to know that if what you're going through is nothing but the devil, you've something on the inside that's working on the outside.

> If what you're going through is nothing but the devil, you've something on the inside that's working on the outside.

But the important thing when we're facing our test with destiny in the storm, in the rain, is to be sure that we stand our ground like Job.

Not only did he lose all of his cattle. Not only did he lose all his land and house. Not only did he lose his sons and daughters. But, even the people that he loved the most were abandoning him because they didn't understand the destiny behind his experiences.

That was probably extremely hurtful. His friends thought he was crazy. His wife thought he should just go ahead and curse God and die. Everybody had turned on him.

Here's the deal → At first, before all of this had happened, people respected his reputation. His reputation was well admired, a rich, noble man who stood strong, steadfast and unmovable to God and God, would, in return, bless him with all that he wanted and needed.

Now, in the eyes of other individuals, he is a man who the devil is after and God is not with and he's doomed for suffering and death. He was now alone.

Isn't it so amazing how people are? First, they can be for you. And the next thing you know they are against you. When everything is going well, you've got support, but when you're really on your knees struggling, hurting in pain, you can't find those same people helping you out.

This is the first time that Job experienced anything like this, but thank God, it did not faze him in any way, shape, form or fashion.

Job didn't even pay attention to his wife. He didn't even pay attention to his friends. He only paid attention to his faith. He only paid attention to his trust in God. He only paid attention to what God had in store for his life. He put God first. He put his confidence first.

He put his trust first. He put his conviction first. He put his belief first. He put his loyalty first. He put his commitment first. So, here it is: his reputation is demolished. He's sick in his body. He's all alone praying, and wondering how long is he going to have to go through what he's going through.

So, he asks God for one thing: He says God I wanna see your face for myself. Don't get me wrong God!

I believe in you. I trust you. I have faith in you. But, I feel like I'd have a little more pep in my step if I was to see you for myself. One thing about Job is that Job knew how to pray. But, not just that.

He knew how to pray with power. And his prayer worked out for him. God came from his throne in heaven to see Job on earth. Job listened to all that God had to say and when it was all over his climax was reached and his test was finished.

You may be stuck between a rock and a hard place. You may be in a situation when your problems seem to weigh you down. You may have circumstances on every hand. But, Just remember there is a destiny behind your experiences.

Chapter 7:

Forgive and Don't Forget, but Learn

Everybody has had their own unique share of experiences – things that they have been through.

Some people have more stories to tell because some have gone through more than others. And we stand with confidence, as Christians, knowing that God allows us to go through things for a reason. We go through them so that in the end we can become stronger than we were before our trial or tribulation when we have reached our breakthrough.

After counseling people for many years, I have come to discover that, what is probably the most difficult test that God will bring forth to you for you to ever encounter in your life is the test of forgiveness. It's not in any way an easy test.

At some point in everyone's life, they have had to face forgiving somebody for something.

Whether it is a direct confront through themselves or an indirect confront through other individuals, everyone has been challenged with the hardship of having to make the decision of whether or not they will forgive or not forgive.

The response to someone's actions towards you is based on you. You can either make three decisions: forgive them and move on, ignore them and move on, or despise them and move on.

Attesting to each one of those has a consequence that can last for the rest of your life. Two are negative and destructive while one is optimistic and constructive. Which is which?

In order to live a life full of self-peace, you must choose the first option, which is to forgive them and move on. And that doesn't even have to necessarily apply to people, for, in fact, it can effectively apply to things.

Anything or anyone who, at any point in your life, has hurt you, or affected you in a way that you did not expect nor desire, you should forgive them.

Even when it seems as if it is the most unrealistic thing to do, you must forgive them. It is not only the right thing to do, but it is also the best thing to do. It is the finest choice to make.

Reasons Why You Should Forgive

There are two reasons why you should forgive.

<u>**The first reason is to better yourself.**</u> **You don't forgive for other people, but you forgive people for you.**

If someone hurt you, you're not forgiving them for them, you are forgiving them for you. Because if you forgive somebody and they don't accept your forgiveness, that's on them and has absolutely nothing to do with you. It is the matter of you actually forgiving those for the purpose of yourself.

When you forgive people, you are bettering your character, you are bettering your charisma, you are bettering your personality, you are bettering yourself as an individual. Because when you do not forgive somebody or something for what they have done to you in your life, the hurt that they brought upon you, then becomes a burden.

It becomes a load; and when something negative becomes a load on your heart, it has a negative effect on you as a whole, which is not something that you want. You begin to walk around with a burden on you that changes the way you talk, act, and live.

It doesn't seem that way from the beginning, but every time that you become reminded of the thing that you haven't forgiven, your heart revamps the same feeling that it had when it actually happened.

Why experience hurt twice?

Why experience hurt three times?

Why experience hurt more than the actual time that it happened?

Why remind yourself of the pain that you had to go through from that person or individual?

Why keep that on your mind?

It is a painful thought and a painful act not to forgive. Forgiving gives you a sense of relief. And that relief might not be felt at the moment of forgiveness but it will be felt at the moment of remembrance.

The second reason why you should forgive is simply because it is the right thing to do with benefits.

It's one of those things that Jesus told us to do. Forgive one another.

It is the right thing to do. It has benefits to it. When you forgive, you feel better.

When you forgive, there are no burdens on you that are holding you back from getting to where God wants you to be. When you forgive, you allow God to use you. When you forgive, you send your enemies the right message. When you forgive………..

The main question is how? How do you forgive?

How Do You Forgive

That is a difficult question to answer and honestly, there is no generic answer that can abundantly apply to this question.

The way that you forgive, all depends on the situation.

Additionally, alone to it depending on the situation, it also depends on the individual. Some people forgive differently from others.

Knowing your own individual forgiveness method is a capacity that you have to gain, either through experience or pre-plan.

The Power of Forgiveness

There is so much power in personal forgiveness.

You will find yourself in a much better situation in the end, when you actually forgive the people or things that you hurt, because there is power in what you're doing. When you forgive the people who have done something to you or the thing that has done something to you, it releases three realms of change and modification that makes things easier:

First, it is a grief relief.

Like I stated above, it's almost like an entire burden is lifted off of you and has entered into the clouds.

You never want anything in your past to stay in your present. Why else is it called the Past? It's called the Past for a reason, so it does not remain in your present. It has passed on and passed by.

Grief is defined as intense sorrow, great sadness, trouble, annoyance or trouble. That can really mean anything.

Anything that has ever had any type of effect on you that promotes any of those things above that define grief must be relieved of in order to move on and live the rest of your life as an individual man or woman of God.

The second realm of change and modification that comes with personal forgiveness is that, by forgiving, you allow God to use you.

The reason why we breathe ever breath, the reason why he take every step, the reason why we do everything that we do, is not for us, but it's for God. We should live hoping that God will use us because if you let him use you, he will.

You just to have to work towards it. Our goals in life should always be based upon God's will, his purpose and plan in our life.

Truthfully, in order for us to live to the fullest, to do what God wants us to do, God has to work through us. In whatever our decisions may be, whatever career that we go into, our family choices, and more, not only should we include God, but we should create a spiritual atmosphere on the inside of us that can use us.

The mere fact is that God cannot dwell in an unclean place, an impure place. What is impure and unclean in the eyes of God when it comes to us, as flesh, are many things, however, when we actually take the time to forgive, the impurities that are within us are moderately washed away because there is no past on the inside of you.

The only thing that is in the innermost of you is God and that now becomes your present, heading on to your future.

The third and final realm of change and modification that comes with personal forgiveness is that, by forgiving, it delivers a message of love.

That is what forgiving is all about. It is about cancelling obligation. It is about excusing somebody. It is about stopping the act of being angry or troubled about something.

The opposite of anger and hatred is love. So, when you forgive you are doing an act of love. And believe it or not, people see that, people notice that.

There's no guarantee that they will react with the same reaction that you do, but they will feel something by what you've done.

Now, the fact is that your act(s) of love through forgiveness may not and probably will not be consistently perceptible among all people. In other words, some people won't like it.

Some people won't receive it. Some people will not act the way that you want them to in reaction to your act of forgiveness. When you turn the other cheek, that person may come forth and do something else, not getting that message again. When you forgive somebody for their actions, you may smile to them, and they may reply with a negative action.

It happens. Because some people do not consent to other people forgiving them.

But, like I said, you don't forgive for other people, you forgive for you.

So, some people are not going to be able to understand why you do what you do, act the way that you do, and live the way that you live.

Some people will not be able to understand how you can do what the bible says and bless those that curse you, love those who hate you, and do good to them that despitefully use you and persecute you; but, you just know that you are living an effective life in Jesus Christ and that's all that matters.

The Ultimate Forgiveness

Jesus did it. We should try to live and be like him the best way that we can. He executed the Ultimate Forgiveness.
I call it Trinity's Love Plan.

Jesus, the son of God, the king of heaven, and the commander of the angels, was not under any sort of obligation.

There was no contractual or vowed duty or responsibility of him to do anything for us. But, Jesus loved us.

So, he arranges with God a plan that they could work with, that Jesus would go down onto and be relinquished of his individual power that was in heaven, relinquish the title master, but on the title servant, take the flesh of a man, and live a normal life.

But, that life had to be perfect. It had to be full of nothing but purities. He would be tempted by the enemy, but he could not give in. He had to remain strong, steadfast, and unmovable. He didn't have the same type of communication with God that he had in heaven.

He had the same type of communication with God that man had on earth. God would give him power that he needed to perform miracles.

At a point, decided by God, he would have to be arrested to world government, be tortured, suffer, and eventually die and not say a mumbling word. This was Trinity's Plan for forgiveness.

And that was a lot for the son of man, the king of kings, the Lord of Lords to do, to know who you are and the power that you have, and still suffer and die for people who do not deserve it. But, thank God he loved us. He was willing to go through all of that just for us to be forgiven.

That is the perfect example of ultimate forgiveness. Jesus had to do what he had to do to get what he needed done, done.

Sometimes, that is what we have to do. When we are on a mission to forgive, we must keep in mind that we have to do what we have to do to make sure that our goal of forgiveness is reached and accomplished. There is a necessity that we forgive.

Don't Forget!

But don't forget! I know you've heard that from so many people: forgive and forget. However, I am against that aspect.

Here is why: If somebody has done something to you that has negatively affected you and it has caused something about you to be a little different. It has caused something about you to be a little unique, or it might have changed your life, or it might have initiated a difference in you, you never want to be in the same situation in the future that you were in the past.

History will repeat itself if you let it. So, don't forget what happened and why it happened. Don't forget your past because you don't want it to be subsisted and breathed again. Keep that in mind for the rest of your life, but let it go, so it doesn't burden or inconvenience your life.

        Forgive, but don't forget, learn!

Chapter 8
He's Still God

Amidst of the many things that go on in our lives, in this world, and in the lives of others, we must recognize and remember that God is still God and he has not changed since he created us in the garden of Eden; even after Adam and Eve messed up when they ate from the tree of knowledge of good and evil.

Noah messed up because he got drunk after the flood was over.

Abraham messed up because he didn't take God's promises seriously.

Moses messed up because God told him to speak to a rock but instead he struck it with his staff.

Samson messed up because he told Delilah after deceiving her before that if he cuts off his hair, he would lose his strength.

David messed up, for he arranged the death of Uriah and he committed the sin of adultery with Bethsheba.

Isaiah messed up because he quoted himself and didn't quote God.

Jonah messed up because God told him to go Ninevah and tell his people to repent of their sins. But, He ran from going and found himself in the belly of a whale.

And there were so many more people and many more things that those people did, but the point is that every time that we messed up, <u>his love sustained the same</u>. Every time we messed up, <u>his grace sustained the same</u>. Every time we messed up, <u>his mercy sustained the same</u>. Every time we messed up, <u>God stayed the same</u>. And know as you read this book that no matter how many times we mess up now, in the present, he still stays the same. **God does not change.**

He hasn't changed since our existence and he will not change because he is immutable.

Immutable is a term that is used to define God as a God that does not change. And because God does not change, that means, everything else that comes with him being who he is does not change.

God's promises do not change!

His promises do not change. His mind does not change. His perfections do not change. And his will does not change.

He's always been the type of God that looks out for his people. God will protect his people. He will not allow anything that is going to damage them permanently to come against them.

If you trust in God, you are his people and he will protect you. God will protect, acknowledge and bless his people. Under any circumstances. Whether he needs to change an entire situation for another to work, he will do just that. Whatever has to be done, it must be done. God will work things out in your favor.

And not only that but God does things in public with purpose. He does it so that people can see How Good of a God He Is through You.

However, in order, for your breakthrough to be as public as your struggle, in order for your deliverance to be as public as your labor, you must put your God more public than your complaining.

You've got to let people know, while you're going through what you're going through, that you still have faith and believe that God's got it all under his control.

RECOGNIZE → He's still God! He hasn't gotten old! He's still got it. He's still able to do the things that he was able to do in the past. So, don't underestimate God based on the Difference of Time. He's Still God.

He hasn't lost any power. He can still part the red sea. He can still turn a rod into a serpent. He can still make water flow from a rock. He can still divide the river of Jordan.

He can still cause walls to tumble down just based on a shout. He can still make the sun and the moon stand still. He can still deliver somebody who's been in a lion's den all night. He can still deliver somebody's who's been in the belly of a whale.

He can still heal the sick. He can still raise the dead. He can still bring you out. It might sound ridiculous for some of those things to happen simply because we're not used to things like that happening.

It would seem as if those things happening would only occur in a figment of your imagination. It would seem like that type of stuff could only happen back in the day when you had Abraham and Isaac, and Moses and Jacob, David and Goliath, and Samson and Elijah, and so forth; but, it does not matter the people, it only matters the God.

And I want you to know, like Tye Tribett says, if he did it before, he can do it again because the same God right now is the same God back then.

He is the Same God.

Not only that, but he gave us a name that's about every name that at the name of Jesus every knee has got to bow and every tongue has got to confess that Jesus Christ is Lord to the glory of God the father. There is so much power in the name of Jesus.

It can break every chain. The name of Jesus is just as powerful today as it was back then. Jesus gave us the power and God gave us the authority to act in that power through that name.

You see there is a difference in general in the faith that Christians had back then to the faith that in general Christians have today. The reasons why the apostles, which were disciples, would go ride or die for Jesus is because they saw him.

They saw him rebuke demons. They saw him heal a paralyzed man. They saw him catch a large number of fish. They saw him calm a stormy sea by just saying Peace Be Still. They saw him heal that woman with the issue of blood. They saw him give sight to the blind.

They saw him feed 5000 people with 5 loaves of bread and two small fish. They saw him walk on water. They saw him raise Lazarus from the dead. They saw him get arrested in the Garden of Gethsemane.

They saw them put a crown of thorns onto his head, beat him with a whip, make him carry his own cross up that hill called Calvary. They saw him nailed to the cross, they saw him say "Father into your hands I commend my spirit."

They saw him, not fall sleep, not slip into a coma, but they saw him die. And saw him, alive once again.

So they were determined, they were strong minded, they were indomitable, that Jesus is who he is, beyond of a shadow of a doubt.

They were more than faithful to the fact that God is who he is. They had faith based on evidential sight. Maximum faith + the name of Jesus = power. I dare you today to have faith like you saw him do it too.

We must have that same faith that the disciples had when they went out and told the world everywhere they went that Jesus is coming back; that he is Lord, he is our Savior, and that if you live in him, you will have power and salvation, you will have authority and deliverance, you will spiritual opportunity and redemption. We must have that same faith that the disciples had that God is God and he will not change.

So, yes we are living in a unique day in time. But, I'm so glad that we are living with a unique type of God. God has not and will not change.

If He Did It Before, he can do it again, because the same God right now, is the same God back then. I want you to know that, with the name of Jesus, God has given us individual power, power to do, as equal as some of the things that they did, some of the miracles that were performed in the bible.

God has given us the power to do anything that we want to do, as long as it is his will and all we have to do is shout the name Jesus.

Live everyday waking up in the morning saying "I've got power."

I've got Power to heal my body when I'm down on my last leg.

I've got Power to encourage myself when I don't have nobody to encourage me for me.

I've got Power to remove my financial situations from my problem lists.

I've got Power to cast out demons and remove demonic influences.

I've got Power to drive haters out of my life.

I've got Power to be delivered from my circumstances and more. All it takes is for me to say the name of Jesus. And he said whatsoever you ask in my name, you shall receive it. God will give it to you. If he did it before, he can do it again, the same God right now is the same God right then.

GOD HAS NOT CHANGED!

God Is Still the God over your problems. God Is Still the God over your enemies. I know that he's still God because he woke me up this morning when I didn't deserve it. I know that he's still God because I'm clothed in my right mind.

We should all know that he's still God because he keeps on blessing us. We should all know that he's still God because he keeps on forgiving us.

He's still God because he keeps on making a way out of no way. He's still God because he protects us from dangers seen and unseen. He still can comfort you when you need uplifting.

He can give you confidence when you're feeling like you're not good enough. He can give you victory in the most defeated situations. He can give you peace to surpass all understanding.

He can help you out just when you need him the most. He can be there for you to call on in the midnight hour. He can wipe ever tear from your eyes. He can be your shelter in the time of a storm. He can be your harmony in the time of confusion. He can be your friend when you're friendless.; your family when you're family less.

Pastor Charles Jenkins said He can move mountains. He can keep you in the valley. He can hide you from the rain. He can heal you when you're broken. He can be your strength when you're weakened. Or like the old folks used to say He can pick you up. He can turn you around. He can place your feet on solid ground. He can heal your body. He can make you strong. He can make you to hold out just a little while longer. He can and he will. He can and will. He can and he will. God is still God. He's not changing any time soon.

Chapter 9
A Personal Relationship With Jesus

There was a moment that we read about in the book of John when Jesus was talking with his disciples.

He was comforting them by talking about heaven. He goes into few details in regards to what exactly they can expect, but he gives small snippets of detailed information about this amazing place, that in every breath we take and step we make, we should try our absolute best to get there by living the best life that we can.

Thomas, one of his disciples, says to him, "We don't know where you are going, so how can we know the way?"

Jesus answered, "I am the way and the truth and the life. No one comes to the Father except through me. If you really know me, you will know my Father as well. From now on, you do know him and have seen him."

Jesus said <u>I AM The Way, The Truth and the Light!</u> The major message that Jesus is expressing in this passage is the fact that he is the way.

He is the way to living an effective life. He is the way to getting into heaven. He is the way to having a connection with God.

It is all through him. In everything that we are, do and live, Jesus is the way. If we need healing, Jesus is the way. If we need deliverance, Jesus is the way. If we need a breakthrough, Jesus is the way. If we need change, Jesus is the way. If we are looking for success, Jesus is the way. To everything, Jesus is the way.

When Adam and Eve ate from the tree of knowledge of good and evil, unfortunately, we lost the special connection that we had with God. He still loved us, as he never stopped and still never stops. But, the type of direct communication that we had with God was no longer our opportunity to experience.

We had paradise and we messed up by not doing what God said do. The garden of Eden was our safe house, meaning to be our eternal land of happiness that we can spend with God. No longer was that the case. But, the joy of Jesus' first coming is that he restored that connection.

> Jesus restored our spiritual connection.

Through him, we had, and have the opportunity to touch God's heart when we sin so that we might be forgiven. It is through him that now we have the opportunity to live eternal life with our God in heaven. All we have to do is live in Jesus.

We hear that phrase all of the time: live in Christ. But, what does that really mean? It means to have a personal relationship with him.

There is a necessity that you have a personal relationship with Jesus. It is the only way that you can live in him, through having a personal relationship. Having a personal relationship means that you know him. It means that you talk to him. It means that he is your friend. It means that he is someone that you feel comfortable with.

So, when you really think about it, having a personal relationship with Jesus Christ is quite similar to having a personal relationship with a human individual. It involves several of the same actions, duties, and inclusions that it would if you were dealing with a really close friend.

There is one difference that allows there to be a unique separation and that is how you sustain that personal relationship with Jesus Christ.

How do you get or maintain a personal relationship with Christ? Through a little something called Prayer. We talked about prayer in the first chapter: the simplicity and the power of it.

Prayer is communication with God. You develop and hold up a personal relationship with Christ through Prayer. The more you pray, the better.

Get to know Jesus, who he is, why he did what he did, and if you really want to be inspired, just think about how you would live your life without him doing what he did.

Read the Word of God, especially the gospels of Jesus Christ, so you can be reminded of the power that you have as an individual.

Know for yourself that Jesus is a true friend who you can call on and talk to in the midnight hour. You can call on him in the morning, noon day, and even in the midnight hour, and he will always answer.

But, what does all of this do for you or to you – having a personal relationship with Jesus? I'll tell you……Having a personal relationship with Jesus Christ has benefits that this world just cannot give you.

First, you will have the opportunity to experience a true ultimate friend. Until we've met Jesus, we don't know what a true friend is. He's always there to talk to (literally).

He can make you feel better when you're ill in any area of your life. He can mend your broken heart. He can be your bread when you're hungry. He can be anything that you need whenever it is that you are in need. Jesus can stand that position in your life. He is a true friend.

The next benefit, for those who are in Christ is that he will create in you a new you. An entire side of you that you don't even know that you have will rise and show. He will live in you.

You won't talk the same way you used to talk. You won't walk the same way you used to walk (figuratively speaking). You won't act the same way that you used to act. You won't do some of the same things you used to do. You will be different in your actions, as result of your reactions.

When people do things to you, you may not react with anger or irritation, the Jesus in you might just get you to the point when you can just smile and "bless those that curse you, love them that hate you, and do good to them that despitefully use you and persecute you."

You will find yourself a totally new person, with brand new experiences, because you see things different than before.

The third benefit and final benefit, though there are more, is you get some extra joy. You should be able to walk into a room and people should be more than able to see the Jesus in you. Because you've got something on the inside working on the outside.

You should be able to bless someone's day that's in a bad mood, just by your smile and your attitude because you have joy. But, not just any kind of Joy – the joy of Jesus Christ. When you know who you are and whose you are, you have an ego – and please know, that as long as you're humble about it and you don't find yourself higher than anyone else, there is absolutely nothing wrong with that.

It's good to have a positive perspective on the things that you have to do endure in life. I don't know about you but I do not find any delight in seeing someone who appears to be in a bad mood all of the time. With Jesus, you have joy because for one, you know that through him you have a higher destination.

That higher destination is a land called heaven. And as, my great-grandfather used to sing "When I get through workin' down here, out in the sunshine or out in the rain, I'm going to live with Jesus. Won't it be grand!"

When you have a personal relationship with Jesus Christ, you have that everlasting joy that resides in your soul, in knowing that life is hard and full of trials and tribulations, enemies and foes, problems and circumstances that must be endured. However, if I just deal with what I have to deal with here on this earth, suffer all that I have to suffer on this earth, endure all that I have to endure on this earth, one day I will be in heaven enjoying glory with the Lord.

Jesus gives us that Joy. He gives us that peace. He gives us that reconciliation. He gives us that gladness. He gives us that encouragement.

So, if you're looking for joy, gain a personal relationship with Jesus Christ. That is the third benefit: you have joy.

I am definitely not going to lie to you and say that it is going to be easy because I will instead tell you the truth by stating that it is not. The reason why is simply because the closer that get to Jesus, the harder it will get in your life, because the devil will know that you've got something about you (Jesus) that is a threat to his plans.

He will try to do his duty which is to steal, kill, and destroy. He will tempt you with temptation and lure, to try to entice you to follow him and the things of this world. He will inflict pain and suffering in your life, so that you can feel discomfort and agony. He will put stumbling blocks in your way to try to prevent you from seeing Jesus, but just know that God will turn your stumbling blocks into stepping stones, if you let him. Know that God can interrupt the plans of the enemy. Don't give up. Stay encouraged that God is with you.

Your personal relationship with Jesus Christ will never be in vain if you don't let it. If you keep your relationship between two and no more, it will be successful, and you will be able to live an effective life in Jesus Christ, that will result in the grand opportunity of living eternally with our father in heaven.

Chapter 10
Let God Fight Your Battles

One of the great conceptualities of life is the thought of and the knowledge that life comes with the fact that battles must be fought.

This concept is applied strongly to those, especially who are Christians, those whose lives are full of faith and belief, those who really trust in the Lord with all their heart and lean not unto their own understanding. This is because these people are the enemy's favorites.

The devil comes to steal, kill, and destroy. Those are his three ultimate purposes.

His mission is to overall demolish the kingdom of God, which are us, his people. So, the devil plans attacks on God's people. But, uniquely, Satan knows exactly who to plan his attacks on.

When you read through the bible, you realize that all of the people who the devil attacked were people who either had a testimony or a testament. He only attacked people that walked with dignity and purpose. He only attacked people who stood with opportunity and destiny. And I want to let you know that his interests have not changed. His goals have not reformed. They are still the same.

If there is somebody who has a vision for success and who never loses faith in their dreams, he/she is a target of the enemy. It will be that person that the devil will attempt at his best to attack because it is those people that are a threat to Satan's goals as the adversary of God.

Do you ever wonder why bad things happen to good people? Do you ever ponder on the fact that sometimes you can be so faithful to God and still experience hurt and pain? Do you ever speculate on the thought on how sometimes when everything starts to go right, out of nowhere, things just start to go wrong?

It is because God allows Satan to tempt us with trials and tribulations, not to weaken us, or make us worse than what we are but instead to strengthen us and to make us stronger than what we are.

When we endure things in life that may last for a long time, they are simply tests. They are examinations that God is observing from his throne in heaven, trying to see how you're going to handle what the enemy can and will throw at you.

There are several battles in life that must be fought. There are several clashes in life that must combat. There are several encounters in life that must be faced and there are several confrontations in life that must dispute.

But, the spirituality of the matter is that, no matter what our physical mind may think, we must allow our spiritual mind to speak, in knowing, that we cannot survive a battle by ourselves. I know that the average notion in the world is that you can do whatever it is that you want to do in life by yourself, independently, but there is a significant add-on to that, because alone that statement will be proven to be ineffective.

You cannot do anything without God. God is the source of your strength. He is the strength of your life. You cannot act without him, nor breathe, walk, talk, or live. He simply is God.

So, think about it: If God is the source of your strength and the strength of your life, YOU NEED HIM to sustain in your physical body a spiritual mind and vessel or physique that will allow you to simply be ready.

When you look at stories like David and Goliath in the bible, you are able to attest without doubt that the Lord will bring you out when you are spiritually ready. When King Saul equipped him with armor and so forth, and David decided to reject them all, Saul did not understand. He did not fully grasp on to the concept that the battle is not yours; it's the Lords when you allow it to be that way. David did just that.

He might not have been physically equipped with what man might find to be sufficient for battle, but he was spiritually equipped with what God knew was adequate for battle and it was because of that, that he was able to fight Goliath and in the end found himself unharmed and most of all delivered.

The mere fact, when you face the odds within the circumstance, is that if David would have entered into the battle spiritually unequipped, his outcome would not have been the same.

I want to feed off of that statement briefly in stating that there are some battles in life that you cannot fight on your own. In those battles, if you were to attempt to fight in them, you would find yourself in a situation when you would become overwhelmed, consumed, and never delivered nor sustained. The battles in life must be turned over to God.

What does that mean?

It doesn't mean that you can just give it to him and just trust and believe in the positivity of its outcome, without putting any type of physical effort…..Because faith without works is dead.

It instead means that you should in all cases and ways bring your hardest battles to God and he will advise you, guide you, and most of all equip you with both the knowledge and the power through his holy spirit to make sure that you are spiritually ready to deal with them.

LET GOD FIGHT YOUR BATTLES!

If you go into a battle that you are not rightfully equipped with, the enemy will attack and scorn you emotionally as well as physically until the point that you will find yourself in a situation that you feel is completely unbearable.

If you go into a battle that you are not rightfully equipped with, the enemy will have partial control over you because there is no type of spiritual blockage or representative stand point on your behalf.

If you go into a battle that you are not rightfully equipped with, you will not prevail, you will fail.

However, if you **do** go into a battle that you are rightfully equipped with, God will prepare a table before you in the presence of your enemies.

If you go into a battle that you are rightfully equipped with, God will allow your shortcomings to become your virtues.

If you go into a battle that you are rightfully equipped with, God will make you the head and not the tail, above and not beneath, a lender and not a borrower.

If you go into a battle that you are rightfully equipped with, God will make sure that you are spiritually ready to come in contact with whatever the enemy will throw against you.

But, that is only if you let God fight your battles. He will equip you. He will prepare you. He will furnish your flesh with the desires of his spirit. Turn your problems, your situations, your inadequacies, your battles over to the Lord and he will work it out!

Chapter 11
Faith In The Right Place
Opportunities Like Never Before

As men and women of God, we have been placed in such opportunistic positions, by which we are able to do exceedingly abundantly above all that we could ever ask or think, according to the power, authority, and honor of God.

The truth is there are no limits to what we are able to do. And thank God, because of him sending his son Jesus into the world to live and to die, there are no obstacles or enemies that have the rank to stand as a threat to the things that we do.

That is the reason why you should always aim high. Limitation should, to the best of our capability, never be a consideration. You should always stand tall. You should always look prohibitive. You should always live each day with the grand phenomenon of truth that greater is coming and that there is something more superior, larger, bigger, and grander than where you are and what you are doing right now.

Even when people think that your thoughts, your dreams, your aspirations are "coo – coo", it takes a mindset to state and, most of all, believe that if that is true, you are "coo-coo" for Jesus.

There is absolutely nothing wrong with dreaming the most imaginative dream. Those type of dreams that contains something that you would inconceivable and unimaginable is not a bad thing to dream. It just takes faith. Jesus said that if you just have faith the size of a mustard seed, you can move mountains.

Do you realize how true this is? Do you recognize how realistic this in your life?

This statement, I'm sure, was not tricky that may impose something different from the message that is plain out delivered.

When Jesus said you could move mountains, he meant that you could move mountains. Think about all of the mountains in your life that you have to face, each and every day.

You may be living pay check to pay check. You may be struggling from one thing and find yourself backed by another. Regardless of what your situation may be, your faith can see you through and your faith can bring you through. It is so significant that we do not, in any way, denote the opportunities that lie within our faith. Faith can do so much in our lives. It's just all about what you have your faith in. ← That is what matters the most.

There are many of us who will have faith and a large amount of it to. Some people have so much faith, they believe in anything that they put their mind to.

They stand strong to the belief that if God brought them to it, he will bring them out of it. Therefore, they don't have any doubt in their mind that what God has in store for them, it is for them. But, they don't have their faith in the right thing. They have their faith in their situation.

Let's Face SPIRITUALITY – Your situation may never work out, but God will always work out.

Your situation can fail, but God will never fail. Your enemies may win, but God will never lose. Your power within your problems may arise, but God will never lose his power.

Your trials may grow, but they'll never get too big for God to handle. The Spirituality of all matters is that situations are invariable, while God stays the same. That is why we must instead put our faith in God.

The main thing to remember is that if we put our faith in our situations, things can go wrong. However, if we put our faith in God, nothing will go wrong. When your faith is in God, he's got it all under control. It's all about putting your faith in the right place.

When you put your faith in God, instead of you praying, asking for God to change your situations or deliver you from your circumstances, you will instead pray that his will be done. When you put your faith in God, you will pray that the Lord will help you and leave everything else alone.

There is power when you put your faith in God. Don't put your faith in your problems - that they'll change, that you'll be delivered from it, because what you want to happen is not always the best thing to happen. The change that you want to be brought forth is not always the change that is meant to be brought forth.

The enemies that you want to leave you alone and be removed from your life are not always the right people to be removed. God is the one who is omnificent, being all knowing. He is the one who knows what is best, what we should do, and how we should do it.

It is because of that, that we should recognize that he is the one who we should put our faith in because when we put our faith in him, we don't have to worry about getting sad, or depressed, or even mad, because things may not go our way; we will instead be acceptable because with faith in God, things go his way.

Faith in God will take you so far. If it is meant to happen, if it is his will -> It will take you beyond limits and past strongholds.

It will deliver you past situations and towards deliverance.

It will take you past enemies and to better friends.

It will move you past difficulties and towards eases.

It will remove you from your current place and put you in a place of authority, liberty, freedom, and justice.

It will push you over restrictions and towards prospects.

Faith in God will get you to where he wants you to be. That is faith in the right place and it is only thing that will lead you to experiencing opportunities like never before.

When I say opportunities, I mean that, and nothing less!

As I stated in the beginning of this chapter, As men and women of God, we have been placed in such opportunistic positions, by which we are able to do exceedingly abundantly above all that we could ever ask or think, according to the power, authority, and honor of God.

All of that comes when we take on the full armor of God, by putting our faith in him, relinquishing ourselves, and putting on a spiritual mindset and body to live in. It is then that we have power. I'm talking about real, true, authentic power.

Not witchcraft, not sorcery, not wizardry, not magic, not enchantment. I'm talking about the Power of God that outweighs all of that. Jesus gave it to us. He gave us the ability to do anything that we need, as long as we act in the name of Jesus and it is the will of God.

We have power; Power through our faith to reach any goal that we want to reach. We have power through our faith to climb any foothill that we want to climb. We have power through our faith to elevate to any highland that we want to get to.

Never look at things that you want to do as unrealistic, no matter how old you are. If you're young, don't think that you're too inexperienced, that you don't have the resources, that you don't have the support.

Have confidence in knowing that God has got your back and that's all that you need. If you're aged, don't think that you're too experienced and that you don't have what you used to have to get to where God wants you to be.

Have confidence in knowing that you have everything that you need and more to get what you need done to get to where God wants you to be.

Never let age be a concern. Never let your past be a concern. If you are somebody who's been to jail, who's been in trouble, who's messed up, the key word is <u>been</u>, being past tense. Allow not your past to stop from your future. Instead, allow your past to influence you to develop a better future.

As long as you put your faith in God, and not your situations, and as long as you leave every decision, every important aspect up to him, allowing him to speak and act through you, everything will work out in your favor, according to how he wants it done.

We don't know what's right or good for us. We don't know if the things that we want to do outside of the spirit is positive or negative.

That is why we lean to God. That is why we live in Jesus, to ensure that we spiritually exist in a safe house by which we can ensure that with faith in him, what's happening in our life is what is supposed to be happening.

Place your faith in God, put your hands in God's hands, and watch God live inside of your heart. It will be then and only then that you will be able to feel for yourself opportunities like never before.

Chapter 12

Be Humble

Don't Forget Your Roots

There is absolutely nothing wrong with being successful.

We were made to be successful in the things that we do. When God made man, he made us in his own image. We were made with a destiny that resembles the spiritual qualities of God.

God is great. We were made in the image of him; therefore, we are destined for greatness. Our destiny can change based on our own decisions and choices. That is why God has made it our personal responsibility to do what we need to do to stay on the right track, to remain on the right path to fulfilling the contents of our destiny.

Our destiny is so valuable and is very vulnerable of being tampered with. Thankfully, Jesus has given us his holy spirit that we can use in order for us to do what we need to do.

That is the reason why success is reasonable and success is acceptable. God wants us to achieve accomplishments in the things that we do. Being blessed is a part of our spiritual genes. It is set on the inside of us. It is a part of how we were made. Therefore, there is no fault in receiving blessings.

Where fault is brought about is when we inaccurately receive our blessings. We have what we have because God decided that he was going to bless us with what we're blessed with.

We must be entirely humble in our response to the blessings that we receive from the Lord.

One of the biggest mistakes that we can ever make after receiving a blessing of any nature is to become big headed. And believe it or not sometimes we can get big headed and we don't even know that we do.

It is just forever important to consistently keep in mind, humility.

Humility is deeply connected to blessings. Blessings are not obligations from God and I'll get into more details about that in another chapter. But, for right now, just know and remember that God is not under any type of obligation for giving us what we have.

There is a reason why we are how we are and why we are who we are as individuals.

Just like trials and tribulations are a test, sometimes so can blessings be as well because sometimes God will bless us with little things, just to see if our heart is ready to receive the big things. One thing about God is that he will not enter us into things that we are not ready to encounter. That is why humility is important. It is what God is looking for as part of your character.

How exactly do you remain humble? That question cannot be defined accurately from me. I can only give you some things to remember, in your daily actions and notions.

First, aim not to compare yourself to other people or other things. The spirituality of the matter of how God created his people is that he does not show favoritism in the general area of love. He loves us all equal. He created us all equal. We must recognize that equality of love amongst all of us – the fact that what makes us unequal is when we make ourselves unequal by the things that we do and the way that we act. However, inequality is only able to be noticed and identified from the eye who initiates it.

Let me give you an example: Diversity is obvious, but its hidden thought and action concepts including racism, prejudice, bigotry, and discrimination are only unleashed by the specific individual. Let's say you enter into a room full of varied individuals of various races and ethnic groups. By sight, you can easily notice the diversity. But, it is not until one individual in that room will identify that diversity and allow that acknowledgement to provoke further philosophies, as stated above: discrimination.

The mere fact is that just like beauty is in the eye of the beholder, so is inequality.

Up in heaven, God looks at us all on an equal standpoint. It's no doubt that he favors us. But, that favor does not in any way come in conflict with the love that he has for us and how he decides to show it. We have to live distinguishing, appreciating, and plain out loving the fact that we are equal.

God loves us all the same. He blesses us differently because though his love is the same for all of us, he has different plans for all of us in our lives. That is why we cannot compare ourselves to others.

The plan that God has for me may not be the same for you. The plan that God has for you may not be the same for somebody else.

God has different plans, different tactics, different strategies, different ideas, different everything for everybody. Though we are all equal, we all live different lives according to God's will.

The only thing that comparing yourself to others does is it allows you to bring further focus on the people that you're comparing yourself to. But, the question is why would you focus on other people more than you focus on yourself?

It takes up entirely too much time. It involves entirely too much work and effort putting your focus, your emphasis, your attention on other individuals, because you are trying to compare yourself to them. The time that you spend doing that can be easy time that you can spend working with what God has given you sustain within where you are or to grow greater than where you are.

Second, Remain Teachable.

Nobody knows everything. Even when you've got to the point when you think that you have experienced the utmost concepts and aspects of life, the realism in life morally affirms that you do not know everything.

Not even seniors and elders know everything. It does not matter what high position that you may have; you still do not know everything.

The only person who knows everything is God. There is not one point in our life when we reach a time when we've grown so large in our life scale that we know everything that we need to know.

One of the largest parts of humility is remaining teachable; being willing to intake knowledge that you receive. Even when you've gotten to a point that you feel safe and secure in life, it can't do you any harm. Here's why: everything you hear, you don't have to listen to. Everything that you listen to, you don't have to pay attention to.

That's the beauty of teaching. It's only extra knowledge that is brought upon you. What you decide to do with that knowledge is your choice.

Remain teachable, because if you don't, you automatically block out knowledge that could be worth receiving.

Don't forget your roots. Just in case you didn't know, where you came from are your roots. It is that that created you who you are.

I see this happen, unfortunately, often in families, where someone will grow into their adult years and spend it with themselves or with their individual families and totally forget about the family that was his family before he didn't have the family that he has.

You can't forget the people or the things that helped you out when you needed it the most. It is your responsibility to give honor where honor is due, simply by being humble about it.

<u>Humility is all that it takes to bask in the holy presence of God.</u> The holy presence of God is so beautiful and it puts you in a position of peace. It puts you in a place of total calmness and tranquility. But, most of all, it puts you in a place of divinity (holiness).

God can you use you more than you could ever imagine when you are humble. When you don't compare yourself to other people or individuals, when you remain teachable to intake information and knowledge, and when you don't forget your roots, God will see that you are ready for greater.

Chapter 13
PRAISE TOWARDS PROGRESS

One of the first sermons that I have ever preached was *"Let Everything That Hath Praise Ye The Lord."* It came out of one of my favorite scriptures: the 150th Psalm, which says..................

(King James Version)

(1) Praise ye the Lord. Praise God in his Sanctuary: praise him in the firmament of his power.

(2) Praise him for his mighty acts; praise him according to his excellent greatness.

(3) Praise him with the sound of the trumpet; praise him with the psaltery and harp.

(4) Praise him with the timbrel and dance; praise him with stringed instruments and organs.

(5) Praise him upon the loud cymbals; praise him upon the high sounding cymbals.

(6) Let Everything that hath breath praise the Lord. Praise ye the Lord. PRAISE THE LORD!

Anybody who has ever been mentored or counseled by me knows that I'm a big person on praise. The main reason for this is because I recognize its power and ability. I know what it can do and I want to take this chapter to let you know too.

Life is full of so many trials and tribulations, so many obstacles and circumstances. The truth is if you don't have some sort of motivation, you will find yourself in a position of crisis and depression. This motivation that you need is praise.

Praising God is so beneficial!

#1 – It can make you feel better.

After you get finished praising and worshipping, you've poured out to him, and gave him your all, you will feel relieved. You will be in a situation when your problems are no longer your worries. You will experience a moment when your enemies are no longer your concerns.

Have you ever gone to church one day and they sang a song that really just hit you? Have you ever been to church one day and there was a praise break that really just got to you? And you left that church feeling much better!

That is no coincidence! It is the power of praise.

Throughout the week, you can face so much at your job with your boss or your colleagues, at home with your family, or just out and about with friends or people period. That is a lot to deal with. Sometimes your day can be so hard and stressful. If you don't let it out, it will stress you out even more. That's where praise comes in handy. You will feel relief. You will be just a little calmer. The more you praise him, the better you will feel.

#2 – It Increases Favor

There is absolutely nothing that we can ever do to deserve the blessings that we receive from God. Every blessing, ever gift, every asset, every advantage – from him waking us up this morning, to him letting you read this book is all due to the enormity of his grace, mercy and favor.

When you praise God, it affects the favor that God has upon your life. The more favor that you have, the more blessings you shall receive and anything "spiritual" that you do, increases your favor.

So, when you pray and when you hope, don't pray just for blessings, pray that God will increase your favor that he has over you.

One big step for you to take is in all circumstances, to take on the responsibility as an individual and give God praise. God appreciates that. In fact, he loves it! God inhabits the praises of all his people!

#3 – It Produces Results

I'm pretty sure you've heard the famous saying "When the praises go up, the blessing some down. And it sure does!

If you really want to see a miracle, praise him for it!

If you really want to see healing, praise him for it!

If you really want to see God make a way completely out of no way, praise him for it!

If you really want to see yourself brought out and brought through your situation, praise him for it.

If you really want to see God in action, doing the many things that we come to read him doing in the bible, praise him for it.

Praise God for your blessings! Praise him for your breakthrough!

Do it in advance! Before you even see it coming, praise God for it. That's when it's able to happen.

Don't let anyone stop you from praising God. That goes for people as well as well as environments.

You have a mission, a goal, a purpose in life. You were created to give praise and worship to God. No one has the right to stop you from praising God.

David danced so much until he was out of his clothes. Many people thought David was crazy, but David had faith in God and trust in what his praise could do.

Praise him your way. Some people holler. Some people put their hands up high. Some people shout. Some people dance. Some people sing. Some people step. And the list continues. But, whatever way applies to you, praise your way through. Progress comes when you praise your way through towards your goals.

Chapter 14

Favor, Grace, and Mercy

We were made to be blessed.

Yes that's right!

Now, this is my opportunity to inform you that God blesses different people in different ways. The way that God blesses you may not be the same way that he blesses me. Vice-versa, it works the same way, in which the way that God blesses me may not be the same way that that God blesses you. Inimitably, God has a unique way of blessing his people, being that this way is influenced by his all knowingness. He knows what blessings are right for certain people.

God loves everybody the same but blesses everyone differently. It is for that reason that we must understand the importance of not comparing ourselves to other individuals and the life that they live.

Though we all live different types of lives, based on the blessings that God chooses to give unto us, we all have it placed in our spiritual genes to be blessed. Within each of us is a genetic factor or material of some sort that has been established for the purpose of being blessed.

You see, God made man, us, out of his own image.

We resemble God: physically, spiritually, and morally. We were made in his image. We were made in his copy, his persona; not even, all in the way that we particularly look, because, both you and I know that we all look different in some manner. But, we were made in a duplicate of his qualities.

If God is great, we were made in greatness. If God is immense, we were made in immensity. If God is magnificent, we were made in magnificence. If God is excellent, we were made in excellence. We were made in the divine image of God.

It is the qualities and the makings of who God is, that are in our spiritual inheritable factors. In our DNA is the opportunity to live with the image of God. We are destined for blessings to enter into and be a part of our life because that is the way that God made us to be.

Yes, Adam and Eve messed up, and it gave us a bad standing in the eyes of God. No longer did we have that same sort of communication that we had with him. But, Jesus came. He came that we might have life more abundantly, through eternity. He came to restore that connection, that communication. We have it back like we used to have it in the past.

In other words, it's not over. God can still use us for his benefits. He can still bless us. That's the good thing. That's the good news. We know it as the gospel.

We are meant to be blessed. It is in our destiny. It is a calling of us all – an ultimate fate that God has placed inside of all of us.

But, in order for us to intake the blessings that God has in store in each and every one of our lives, we must first develop a full understanding of the concept of blessings.

A clear perception must be gained of why you have what you have and why you're blessed the way that you are.

Sometimes, we can be thrown so many blessings at one time, as simple as waking up in the morning and being able to breath, experiencing a brand new day, and forget the fact that these opportunities given by God are complimentary, not obligations.

There is absolutely nothing that we have done nor is there anything that we can do to deserve the blessings that God has bestowed into and upon our lives.

It is so easy for us to get into the habit of doing something good and expecting to spiritually get something back as a duty or responsibility of God.

You see, it is often thought that it is the things that we do or the accolades that we gain that "obligates" God to having to do something for us. Often times we think that it is the success that we attain that necessitates God to have to do something for us. Often times, we take phrases such as when the Praises Go Up, The Blessings Shall Come Down and instead of looking at it as "If we praise God, if it is his will, and in his favor on our life, the blessings will come down," we can sometimes look at it as "if we praise God, God has to send down some blessings."

Face the reality – God is God. He doesn't have to do anything for anybody else. He does not have to allow us to experience the days and involvements that we undergo. But, him doing that would be against his character. Who is God? God is a loving God. Who is God? He is a caring God.

If he doesn't do anything else for us, not only has he already done enough, but he is not obligated to having to do anything else for us.

There are three sources that lie as determination for the blessings that we have.

Every blessing that we have is because of God's <u>GRACE, HIS MERCY, and HIS FAVOR.</u>

Those are the three things that determine whether we have what we have.

Now, **grace** is impervious and untouchable. You cannot affect that. It is something that God has placed generally in our lives to save us, to keep us, to ensure that we don't fall off of the right path with him. Grace also stands as an outlet of support. All have sinned and fallen short of the glory of God at some point in their life. Grace is something that God gives you to pick you up when you're down. It's there to place your feet on a solid ground that you need.

Mercy is the same way. It is the opportunity concept. We can't affect that as well.

But, there is one thing that you can affect and that is your favor.

Well, what about everything else: faith, patience, trust, commitment, courage, obedience? Aren't those all things that determine blessings too? What about praise?

If I praise God, isn't that something that determines my blessings too? Well, no. All of those things are what you call assets.

They are assets because those are things that affect your favor. They can increase the favor that God has upon your life. Favor is a great thing to have. It benefits you. It aids you. It helps you and everybody needs some help.

The greater faith that you have, the more favor you will have. The more patience that you have, the more favor that you have. The more trust that you have, the more favor that you have. The more commitment that you have, the more favor that you have. The more courage that you have, the more favor that you have. The more obedience that you have, the more favor that you have. The more praise that you have, the more favor that you have. The more of anything that you do, it increase the Favor that God has upon your life.

And the more favor that you have, the bigger the floodgates of heaven will open up and pour you out a blessing that you won't have room to receive. The more favor that you have, the greater your opportunity to receive your deliverance, to receive your breakthrough, to receive your blessing. It is for that reason that you should aim each and every day to increase the Favor of God that he has upon your life.

Your blessings are not in your actions, your blessings are not in your successes, your blessings are not how much you pray, or how much you come to church. Your blessings are in your favor. Aim to achieve favor over your life by the things that you do.

Chapter 15

You Can Make It

Everyone has their own share of trials and tribulations, obstacles, and impediments, difficulties, and circumstances. That's right! It is that that makes you different – being an individual in your own right and authority.

It is in the will of God to have to go through things, regardless of who you are, what you may do, or where you may come from.

The good thing about the things that we endure in life is that they are temporary.

And truthfully, that temporary status might last for a pretty long time.

But, there is a guarantee from God that there is no permanence. At some point in your life you will reach another level from where you are. Opportunity is in your future. Prospect is in your future. Magnitude is in your future. Distinction is in your future.

1 Corinthians 10:13 says "He will not suffer you to be tempted above that ye are able."

I'm sure you've heard the statement "He will never put more on you than you can bear."

And that is nothing but the truth.

We go through the things that we go through because he allows us to go through them. Nothing that we go through or experience in life catches God by surprise. He has the best interest and the best plans in mind that he instills into us. We must trust and believe in the deliverance that God has destined upon our life.

The fact is that **YOU CAN MAKE IT!** <u>Life is in God's hands.</u> Therefore, you have control over it. There is no doubt that life is no easy task to contract with but God has given you everything that you need to live an effective life with Jesus Christ.

So, I charge you today to, not just exist, but to live your life. Tomorrow is not promised to any of us. Never exist in the past. Anticipate the future. But dwell in the present with joy, peace, happiness, gratefulness – standing on the mighty promises of God. I charge you to stand strong, steadfast, and unmovable. Do not allow anyone to question your faith in God.

Continue to pray without ceasing.

Continue to believe beyond a shadow of a doubt.

Continue to have faith larger than a mustard seed.

Continue to be patient amidst of waiting.

Continue to be committed to God and his word, even when other people have doubted him.

Continue to have courage in him to fight against anything in life that you may face.

Keep on going to church and most importantly, keep on praising the Lord!

Regardless of what state in life that you are in, there is always something to smile about. As long as you still have breath in your body, you are still blessed! Live each day like it!

You do not belong to this world. You belong to God!

About Minister Jared Sawyer Jr.

Internationally and virally acclaimed Minister, Singer, Musician, and Author, Jared Sawyer Jr. is a worldwide sensation of a true man of God with many gifts. Minister Jared Sawyer Jr. is an associate minister at the Center Hill Baptist Church in Atlanta, Georgia, where the Reverend Waymon A. Martin, Sr. is the Pastor. He is the President and Senior Adviser of Jared Sawyer Jr. Ministries, a wide-ministry devoted to "life, family, fun, and faith."

Because of God's grace, Jared has been able to be on the Frank Ski and Wanda Morning Show, BBC Broadcasting's Company, Fox 5, ABC Nightline, and many other media programs. He has been given the opportunity of speaking at numerous events for the NAACP, the City of Stone Mountain, National Black MBA, and more. He has had the honor of meeting, associating, and becoming friends with those as Fred Hammond, William Murphy, Donnie McClurkin, Luther Barnes, Mary Mary, Tony Vaughn, Donald Lawrence, J. Moss, Leland Jones, Shirley Caesar, Producer Will Packer, Mo Ivory, and many more actors, gospel and secular artists, and public figures.

Even though he has gotten the opportunity to meet a lot of people, none of them are more important to him than God. Jared is now 15 years old and the number one thing on his mind is preaching the Word of God. Jared's motto is "Praise Is What I Do"! and I know that God placed him on this Earth to do just that.

For more information on Minister Jared Sawyer Jr., please visit his website at www.jaredsawyerjr.com .

STAY IN TOUCH WITH MY MINISTRY!

FACEBOOK
Like my Facebook Page under
"Minister Jared Sawyer Jr."

TWITTER
Follow me @JaredSawyerJr

YOUTUBE
JaredSawyerJrTV Channel

INSTAGRAM
Follow me @preachjared

WEBSITE
www.jaredsawyerjr.com

Email us at info@jaredsawyerjr.com to be added to my email list.

© Copyright 2013 Jared Sawyer Jr

Made in the USA
Charleston, SC
08 December 2014